# Always Time for Coffee

### A Down-to-Earth Guide for Frontline Managers, Team Leaders and Supervisors

## Kate Minchin

Always Time for Coffee: A Down-to-Earth Guide for Frontline Managers, Team Leaders and Supervisors
© Kate Minchin, 2019
The right of Kate Minchin to be identified as the author of this Work has been asserted in accordance with sections 77 and 78 of the Copyright, Designs and Patents Act 1988.

ISBN: 978-1-7335619-0-7 (print)

Cover design: Stuart Bache
Author photo credit: Nicki Fietzer
Formatting: Polgarus Studio

For Sue, with love

# Contents

# Foreword

Kate and I worked together at Historic Royal Palaces for several years. I was CEO from 2003–17, and for part of that time Kate led frontline teams at Hampton Court Palace, welcoming hundreds of thousands of visitors every year. Subsequently, our paths diverged as she went off first to the University of Oxford, then on to her new adventure in the USA, while I brought my full-time professional career to a close on retirement in 2017. But I always kept a strong memory of Kate as a dedicated and gifted manager who had achieved real, sustained change in a demanding setting. So when, inevitably, she invited me for a coffee to talk about the book and to reflect on managing people, I was delighted to accept.

I spent the first nine years of my working life after university learning how to be a curator. At that time, museums were not natural hotbeds of great management practice. Many of those who had managerial or supervisory responsibility were reluctant practitioners, or ignored it altogether. When I was 30, I got my first managerial role at Ironbridge Gorge Museum. Within a few months, there were 150 people in the organisational chart under my name. At that point I had no proper training, and my only role models were negative ones. I knew what it felt like to be managed badly, and I could only imagine what the opposite to this would look like.

On reflection, the most important transition was to accept the challenge of 'I am a manager' – and it's a pretty scary thought. Most people don't go through childhood and adolescence saying: 'When I grow up, I want to be a manager.' But when you find yourself in that role, you have to relish all that it means. You can't do it reluctantly or half-heartedly. You might do it badly sometimes, and get it wrong – that is part of what it all means – but you have to want to do it.

I have also come to understand that management – along with its bedfellow, leadership – is a lifelong learning process, and this requires being in constant reflection with yourself. It means actively managing your team (collectively and individually), always being aware of the different choices you (can) make and their consequences, and learning for the next time. The wisdom of others is a crucial part in all of this. Whatever situation you find yourself in, you can be sure that someone will have been there before, and their perspective might help you.

There are thousands of books on management – most with important things to say – so why does the world need another one? Why should you pick up this one and invest your time and attention in it?

Kate's book is born of hard-won experience. It is immensely practical and applicable: not a book written by some lofty CEO who has forgotten what it is really like to manage on the frontline, but the cumulative wisdom of someone who has been there and done it year-in, year-out and delivered results. Throughout, she has generously seasoned it with others' insights too: stories that hold wisdom.

In reading it, lots stood out for me – but this perhaps above all:

> Your own development is a career-long project: every piece of work, every project, every conversation is an opportunity to learn and develop. The important thing is taking the time to reflect, and to increase the benefit that you can gain from all the hard work you are putting in on a day-to-day basis.

If you have read even this far, I'm assuming you are ready to take the trip through Kate's fine book, always reflecting on your own experience and working out how to keep developing as a manager, for all the rewards that it brings for your organisation, your team and for you personally.

Keep sharing a coffee, and go well.

Michael Day, CVO

# Introduction

Frontline managers are often neglected when it comes to training and support. In a *Harvard Business Review* survey, 77% of respondents said that frontline managers were important in helping them reach their business goals, and 78% said that they had an important role in achieving a high level of customer satisfaction. However, only 12% said their organisations invested sufficiently in the development of frontline managers.[1] This is a significant mismatch, and yet one that is all too familiar to frontline managers like yourself.

You are clearly in an important role: you are the first tier of management in your organisation, and responsible for many of the day-to-day operations. Some would call you the 'managerial foot soldiers'. You are responsible for a huge team of retail assistants or factory machinists, perhaps a small team of trainers or baristas. You could even have responsibility for a couple of assistant managers. Your title could be anything from 'team manager' or 'team leader', to 'coordinator' or 'supervisor' – I have

---

[1] Harvard Business Review (2014) *Frontline Managers: Are They Given the Leadership Tools to Succeed?*, analytic services report.

even come across 'directors' at this level. No matter what the title on your business card, your role is critical: you bear the responsibility for the performance of a team, and are held accountable for their successes and failures.

I was always on the lookout for books to recommend to my frontline management teams that were specifically targeted at them. I found a few that, although not directly targeted at frontline managers, were useful (I have listed them at the end of this book), but I was always crestfallen by how limited the choice is. So, despite the importance of your job, if you start looking for practical guidance on the shelves of a bookstore, you are likely to be disappointed.

Management books are usually written by people who have not worked in the first tier of management for decades, or in some cases, have never managed a team in their life. I have spent more than 20 years managing frontline teams and their managers. Regardless of the size of the team, the problems I encountered have been the same. I have stressed over staffing numbers, been called on to deal with leaking roofs, had to calm irate customers, all the while controlling my inbox and attending countless meetings.

Most books will present you with overwhelming data and tell you about the latest management techniques: case study after case study based on the practices of internationally renowned, billion-dollar companies. Stories tend to focus on individuals who went on to become president of their company, and now appear in lists of the world's top 50 most successful directors under 30.

This type of information has its value, but how does it help those of us working in the trenches? The latest trendy management programme or buzzwords are of little help when faced with a dwindling budget, demands for new uniform, another difficult conversation with a team member, or an unforeseen crisis meaning that once again you have to miss out on dinner with friends. You don't have the energy to go home, pull out a notebook and pen and pour over the latest management textbook for hours. Wouldn't it be easier just to go for a coffee (or your beverage of choice) with someone who 'gets it'? Who has been in your shoes and managed people in your position for a long time?

Well, I have not only been in the shoes of a frontline manager, I've worn the soles clean off them! I know how valuable your time is, so in this book I will cover the essentials via an honest, down-to-earth 'chat'.

Some of you will be new to all this: after all, this is a tier of management where most people start off. However, some of you will have been doing this for years, and just want to brush up on your skills or check that you are not losing your mind. I will talk about some of the common problems that I have watched frontline managers struggle with, and how I have supported them. I will tell you about some of my own experiences (which I refer to as 'Tales over Coffee' throughout the book): what I got right, what I got wrong, and what I wish people had told me in the early days of my career. For those who have been managing people for a while, hopefully this book will serve as a chance to take stock, go back to basics and be a bit of a refresher. This book isn't about getting you to the top of the career ladder in the least amount of time; but if your concern is being the best possible manager you can, you are in the right place.

For the record: I am not the perfect manager, and I don't claim to have all the answers. But I have been doing this for more than 20 years, hands-on, day-in, day-out: attending the kind of training courses I mention, dealing with the problems I describe, supporting frontline managers and watching them grow and flourish in their careers.

Many years ago I trained as a teacher, so education in one form or another has always motivated me. I would happily send my managers off on training courses, but there was always something missing. The essential aspects of a manager's role were not being discussed, and it pained me to see the same avoidable errors being made time after time, as well as missed opportunities. I wanted my team to realise that making mistakes is OK, that taking time out to reflect on their work is essential and needs to be prioritised, and that 'disruptive' staff can actually be really helpful, if managed in the right way.

During the research for this book I interviewed frontline managers who are doing the job now in Australia, the UK and the USA: some were new to the role, while others have been doing it for years. I spoke to people who manage frontline managers, and those who work with them on a daily basis (I have changed some names and concealed the identity of the organisations they worked for, in order to protect their anonymity). But every case study, quote and story is true, and based on the experience of others or myself. So really, you are getting to have coffee with, and benefit from, the experience of a large number of people.

Why my obsession with coffee and meeting in cafes? It stems partly from frontline managers' lack of private office space and trying to find somewhere where we can be undisturbed when we meet (also partly from my own need for caffeine in order to function at the start of the day, so I save time and combine the two!). I find the buzz and activity of a cafe a creative environment in which to enjoy batting ideas back and forth, exploring possible projects and engaging in original conversation.

Using cafes to meet and discuss business is nothing new. Coffee houses started in the Middle East in the 1500s, and were largely a place for political gatherings, sometimes referred to as 'Schools of the Wise'. Move forward to the 17th and 18th centuries, and the coffee houses of England saw men (that's right, men only – women were not allowed) meet to discuss business and politics. These English coffee houses became known as 'penny universities' in recognition of their reputation as places of learning and the penny paid to enter. Poetry was discussed, scientific experiments carried out and revolutions planned. So really, I am simply continuing a tradition that is hundreds of years old.

The reality is that managing people can be messy and complicated, there are no easy answers. Some days will be hellish, and you will wonder why on earth you are doing it. But you will also have amazing days when you can't imagine doing anything else: when you are full of pride and your ears ring with the sound of laughter, and your teams are enjoying each other's company; when the successes come rolling in and you feel like you can achieve anything with this amazing group of people. It is those days that you do this for: the days when a customer tells you how you made their day, when a team member thanks you for supporting them. These good days will far outweigh the bad, especially when you create an environment in which positivity and success can thrive.

Frontline managers usually manage the biggest teams: teams that are the face of the organisation. Whether that is retail staff or a group of engineers, they are the ones dealing with clients and customers, or making the crazy ideas that others come up with a reality. Yet in many organisations, the big training bucks are spent on executive-level and middle management – the week-long residential courses at prestigious management schools, the seminars and guest speakers, conferences and networking events. While all these are going on, frontline managers are back at the factory, museum, shop or office, making sure that business as usual continues and that there are no crises for senior managers to return to. If they are lucky, frontline managers will get half a day's in-house training once a year.

Of course there are exceptions to every rule, and I am very familiar with a number of organisations that run extensive, good-quality training for frontline managers. However, they really are the exception and, more often than not, while the training is very good, it doesn't quite respond to the frontline manager's needs.

I recall a session on time management that I attended. The trainer acknowledged and worked to the reality that a lot of frontline managers carry radios that they have to respond to immediately. I was blown away – I had never come across that level of awareness before, and haven't encountered it since. Then there are the small companies where there are perhaps one or two frontline managers who don't get a moment's training: perhaps they don't realise that they should be getting some – and even if they do, they have no idea where to start looking.

I hope in some small way to help plug that gap: to give frontline managers a place to start, or the reassurance that they are on the right track.

I want to make it easy. I want to have coffee with you, talk you through some of the stuff that sounds simple but is often neglected. I will take you through some of the things that underpin the work of a good frontline manager. None of it needs corporate jargon or pages of graphs; just a coffee or two with someone who has been there.

Now, what would you like to drink? It's on me!

# 1
# Managing People

## Introduction

If you are already a frontline manager, then I am guessing that your team members are simultaneously the best thing about your job and, on some days, the most challenging thing about it. This might sound harsh, but the reality is that people are demanding. What works for one won't work for another, and everyone can be unpredictable (I know for a fact that I have given my line managers a few headaches over the years).

What about your team members, what do they think of you?

Frances Sampayo, a frontline manager I have watched grow and develop over the years, sums it up brilliantly: 'You're a psychiatrist, life coach, guru, keeper of all answers, solver of all problems and reasons for all problems.' There will be days when they think you can walk on water (admittedly, there are fewer of those), and days when you just cannot get it right (mainly days like this).

So, why do we do it? Why do we put ourselves through the daily challenge of trying to support a large group of shifting personalities, while simultaneously fending off the demands of senior management and customers? For me, it's about pulling together as a team when things go wrong, and the euphoria when you fix problems. It's about watching people challenge themselves and achieve great things, knowing I have been able to support them in some way. It's the laughter in the office, problem-solving with a group of creative minds; it's the predictability and unpredictability of human behaviour, and being surprised by both. It's bouncing back from the disappointment of a team member's poor attitude, as one of their colleagues impresses you with a stellar performance. Some of the most challenging teams to manage are the ones that have given me the greatest pride.

For a frontline manager, the team of people you manage will take up most of your time. Even the most passionate, high-achieving team can be hugely demanding. But if you are clear about your expectations and remain consistent in your responses, you will be halfway there.

If all of this sounds familiar and you feel that you are managing things well, that's fantastic – but do take the chance to reflect on and review your own performance (more on this in Chapter 5). For example:

- Where do you need to up your game?
- Do you need to refocus your energy?

- Is there a problem you keep pushing to the end of your to-do list, but now it is time to tackle head-on?

Your teams will always keep you on your toes, and being a step ahead is something you will have to fight to make time for every day. Put in the effort, and you will find that the days you come home thinking that your team is the best thing about your job will increase, and the amount of times you think you need a lie down to recover from their latest antics will decline.

## Managing passionate people

This might seem a little strange, but one of the hardest (yet equally exciting and rewarding) things I have found to manage is passion. An enthusiastic, dedicated team sounds perfect, but if that energy is not given appropriate outlets or truly appreciated, you have a challenge on your hands.

A passionate, excited team is a wonderful thing. That is what you want, and should strive to achieve – but enthusiasm needs to be given a sense of direction. Your team should feel that you are engaged with and appreciative of their passion, and be able to trust you to capture and harness it. You also need to show and share your own drive with them. Getting them there can be hard work – and once there, they need constant care and attention – but the results are more than worth it. Once you have all of that in place, a passionate team is indeed all the fabulous things you imagine them to be, and you really can achieve incredible things.

## Case Study

Vikki van Someren, Co-founder and Events Director of The Bike Shed in London – an amazing restaurant, bar, shop and venue that is all about motorbikes and their riders – is one of the most passionate and energetic managers I have come across. It is clear that she and her husband, Dutch, manage an organisation made up of passionate people who are full of ideas. So how does that happen, and what pitfalls should be avoided?

'I've always been a passionate person, and I love to be able to express that – it's then that I'm at my most productive and creative. I also know that my levels of enthusiasm can be impacted on by those around me, including my previous managers.

So now I'm running an organisation, I reflect that experience in my own management style and the advice I give to our supervisors and team leaders. I know that if the people running teams are restricted in the workplace, then they equally can't give their teams the opportunity to be passionate and creative. But if they are bubbling over with ideas, totally free in their style and let everyone do what they want, then that passion becomes uncontrollable, so you have to direct team members and help them get the balance right.

You need to give feedback really quickly. Here the guys come up with these really wonderful, crazy ideas, and sometimes I've got to nip it in the bud and say: 'You know what? It's a great idea, but it won't work for us for these reasons.' You give them guidance by putting little stakes in the ground – that way they can navigate their way through their ideas and the needs of the business without putting out their fire.

If you don't offer guidance and you open it all up, the team members get completely lost and overwhelmed – that's when staff don't have any direction, and they start losing the will to live because everything becomes too much.

On the other hand, you can't be too small in your thinking: you can't restrict them too much, because then you won't do anything. Being fluid, giving feedback and guidance, can help drive them and direct that passion.'

Vikki wears her passion on her sleeve and it is contagious and inspiring, which is another important factor. Let the team see your passion, even if it veers off course sometimes and you need to pull yourself back within those 'stakes' that Vikki talked about. Let the team know what drives and excites you. Celebrate success openly, and allow them to see that you get frustrated when something you have all been striving for doesn't turn out the way you had hoped. Let them see that you are human.

When your team sees that you hold yourself to the same standards that you hold them to, they will know it's OK to show their own passion and excitement. They will celebrate the highs with you and commiserate the lows, and you will be a great team.

Sometimes passion can show itself in less obvious ways, and you have to identify it for what it really is. Sometimes it can be hiding in the most negative, challenging behaviour; but if you can spot what's happening, you can work to turn that energy into a hugely productive force for good.

## Case Study

Keith, an operations manager for a large retail operation, took on the job of managing a troublesome team. In his situation, all the negatives were hiding something which, if harnessed, could (and did) do amazing things.

'Some years ago I took over the management of a large team with a poor reputation. They were negative and would complain to other departments, the CEO and even the customers. They were deeply suspicious of management, and resented any change.

I spent a lot of time in conversation with both individuals and groups – they were full of ideas and complaints and, as far as they were concerned, they knew all the answers, despite not always knowing the history, politics or budgetary restrictions. But I kept listening and eventually I realised that it wasn't just that they "knew better", they wanted "it" to "be better". They wanted things to go well, to see improvements and ensure that our customers had a great experience.

The problem was, they didn't know how to communicate in a way that meant they could get people on-side – and didn't know who the best person to talk to was. No one had been feeding back to them, or helping them take on board information that might not be what they wanted to hear. No one had helped them to develop these skills. The shame of it was, they were deeply passionate – they cared, and they had some great ideas.

So, we gave them clear channels to communicate their ideas and concerns. We always responded, and we were always honest. If we couldn't action their ideas, we'd tell them why. If someone simply moaned, it would be explained to them how unhelpful and unproductive that was. If they complained about company policy to the customers, they were spoken to. Over time, the complainers realised how unproductive their approach was, and that those who engaged appropriately were getting responses – and sometimes seeing their suggestions come to fruition.

It wasn't that we didn't want people to have a negative opinion; we just needed to hear it in a productive way. When I first started managing this team, other departments wanted little to do with them. By the time I moved on, other departments were really keen to have one of them on their project committee, or consult with them on proposed changes. They became known as dedicated, switched-on professionals who had invaluable insight that came from being on the frontline of the organisation.'

Be aware that all these fundamentally positive qualities might look like something completely different if they are not kept in check. Just give a bit of thought to what might be motivating and influencing certain behaviours: once you identify them for what they are, then you need to give them an outlet. Make sure that you are all heading in the same direction, and put some stakes in the ground. There is little better than a team of people buzzing with ideas who have the skills to turn them into an exciting reality.

## Don't jump to conclusions

'Have you got a minute?' How much do you dread those words? Not just because you know whatever is coming will take a lot more than a minute of your time, but because that request is going to send you down a rabbit hole that doesn't lead you to anything as fun as a mad hatter's tea party. Instead, you are going to spend the next 30 minutes hearing the story of someone's potentially childish, irritating and possibly even unprofessional behaviour. You can feel the frustration starting to bubble up as you listen to them, your shoulders hunching up towards your ears – but you still hear yourself saying: 'Leave it with me, I'll sort it out.'

Before you march out the door to go and find the culprit, or pick up the phone to human resources and prepare them for the worst, just take a little time to let what you have just heard percolate.

If there is one thing I have learned, it is: don't assume the worst. If you don't handle this kind of situation right, *you* might end up being in the wrong. As we are often told, there are two sides to every story. Dive in based on initial reports, and you might find yourself looking silly – so it's better to calmly gather the facts, rather than jumping to conclusions. Even if you think you are on pretty solid ground because you saw someone behave badly with your own eyes, just stop and take a breath. You might find that someone has indeed done something daft, but by the end of the investigation you will have a much greater understanding of what was motivating their behaviour, that ultimately the company is providing them with support, and that you are empathising with them.

There is no escaping the fact that people do crazy (and sometimes criminal) things in the workplace, and you will find yourself disciplining those concerned (it always amazes me when staff in these scenarios get annoyed at management; after all, they have put themselves in that situation!). However, just as often you will find a backstory, which results in you having to change your approach – especially if the poor behaviour is out of character. There is a range of possibilities you might need to investigate, such as:

- Are they under undue stress at work?
- Are they being bullied?
- Have frustrations come to the surface because they are struggling with the job and need more training and support?
- Are they acting up because of health issues? Are they unwell and had a change in medication?
- What about personal stresses: has there been bereavement in the family? Have they separated from a

partner? Do they have financial or legal problems?

- Are they the main caregiver for a loved one as well as trying to hold down a job?

People can behave in a number of ways when under stress or unhappy, and you need to be sure that neither you as their manager, or the company itself, are responsible in some way. How much of this is your responsibility to deal with? If the problem is work-related, then it is absolutely your responsibility. It is your job to sit down with them, figure out what they need, and provide training or other support. If that works and they get back on track, you then need to spend some time reflecting on how you can do your best to prevent the issue from coming up again:

- How often are you checking in with your team?
- Are you holding regular 1-2-1 meetings with each team member?
- Are you providing enough training for everyone?
- Have you cultivated a culture where people feel that they can come to you if they are struggling, or are you the unapproachable 'scary' manager?

If the problem is health-related or there are issues outside of work, do ensure that they can take the time off to go to a doctor or other relevant appointments. Moreover, be sure to consider these factors:

- What employee resources does your company have available?

- Do they need some time off, or to go part-time for a while?

This is one of the vast, grey areas of management: you can't prepare for every eventuality because the list of possibilities is endless, as are the possible resolutions. Bear in mind that sometimes these things can't be solved, but they can be eased. Equally, I am not saying that some sort of performance management action isn't required if the incident is severe enough; it might just need to be done in parallel with other support. Should your support be endless? No, not at all. There are limits, and at the end of the day you are operating within a business.

Managing people means having an interest in people. You should care about their well-being, and want to help and support them (within reason). This might sound obvious, but you would be amazed by how many managers seem to dislike this part of their role, or get frustrated by people-related problems. Yes, they can annoy you, and you would rather stick a fork in your eye than have another conversation with Bob, Emma or whoever is your current bête noire – that is only to be expected, as a species we can be pretty annoying, all of us! But there is also great pleasure to be gained from seeing your team succeed, and watching individuals carry out incredible performance u-turns with your support.

The requirements and expectation to support and look after staff can vary from country to country, organisation to organisation, and even in the eyes of the law. However, this is not about what is legally necessary (although of course you do have to make sure that you are meeting those requirements), it's about what is morally responsible – what you should do as a decent human being and manager. If you want loyalty, commitment, fun and success, let your staff know that you care. Treat them like the wonderful, flawed human beings they are. There will still be times when showing someone the door is the right and only option, but at least you can be sure that you have done everything you could within reason – and limited the chance of karma getting its revenge on you in the future.

## When 'personality' becomes problematic

Have you ever come across team members who are rude to you? Or maybe you can't quite put your finger on it, something is just 'off' with them? They might be sarcastic or monosyllabic. When you raise it with colleagues, you get comments such as: 'Oh, that's just Chris, don't take it to heart.' I have even heard: 'That's just the way it is when you manage people – you have to deal with their personalities.'

This is no more than an excuse: a way for managers to avoid a difficult conversation or challenging but important part of their job. Unfortunately, avoiding the issue can mean that the team member is not given the support they need to improve and flourish. There is a difference between personality quirks and plain bad manners – we might not always like our colleagues or managers, but we should always behave respectfully towards them.

## Case Study

Marcus was an intelligent, capable team member at a haulage firm, but he clearly lacked respect for management. He wore it like a badge of honour and would look at his supervisors with disdain: responses to questions came across as rude and sneering, no matter how polite or reasonable his supervisors tried to be.

However, even they would say: 'That's just Marcus, it's just how he is – don't worry about it, don't take it personally.' This continued for a number of years, and his negative reputation grew.

When a new head of department arrived, their concern lay not with Marcus, but with the supervisors' response. In the manager's view it wasn't 'just' his personality – he was being disrespectful and unprofessional. It was fine for Marcus to be annoyed with the supervisors if there was just cause, but he should still be polite and work with them to resolve problems in a professional way.

While his poor attitude continued, Marcus was losing the respect of all around him – and he was being let down by his supervisors. It took time, and Marcus hated being confronted, but with the guidance and support of their new manager, the supervisors learned how to respond to his behaviour. It had been sad to see Marcus's talent so sorely misdirected and previously unmanaged, but over time he came to respect the supervisors.

His skills and attitude improved immeasurably, and he gained the respect of his colleagues. It wasn't long until he began to take more interest in the work of the management team and even became an acting supervisor himself, helping when they were short-staffed and supporting them in their daily work.

The early stages of managing Marcus and his attitude were challenging and sometimes painful, but the pay-off for Marcus, the team and the company was more than worth it.

It is not only team members that get away with poor performance hiding behind the defence of 'personality'. It can happen all the way through organisations – which is a shame, as those higher up really ought to be leading by example. However, this is where you come in and set the standards for your own teams. Don't worry about what everyone else is doing; just focus on making sure that you and your team are a shining example (more on this in Chapter 2).

**Case Study**

Louise was a director with a number of staff reporting in to her. Initially employed for her technical knowledge and then promoted, she was now managing people. However, she was struggling with the job: she never did performance reviews, never met for 1-2-1s with her team members, and never thanked, supported or developed them.

Louise's communication with colleagues, written and verbal, was rude, unsupportive and so unprofessional that they didn't know whether to laugh or cry. Her technical knowledge wasn't kept up-to-date, and she was no longer considered an expert in her field. Her performance and reputation were crashing through the floor.

Some of her colleagues (including some more senior) would say: 'Oh, it's just Louise, that's just her style', or 'Well, everyone is different – that's just the way it is when you work with people'. Someone else commented, 'She's been with the company from the early days, the CEO will never let her go.'

The fact that Louise had a hard-working, self-driven team was entirely through luck rather than design, which ensured that her department was not failing miserably. No one, let alone her manager, was prepared to do the challenging job of managing her performance, and the results were impacting on both the individuals around her and the company as a whole.

Louise's colleagues and team members questioned their own hard work and dedication, wondering why they were putting in so much effort. Those who should have been managing Louise lost respect from many in the company. Even people from outside the organisation within the industry were questioning the standards within the company.

What was the result for Louise? Once passionate and knowledgeable, she had become demotivated and directionless, with no encouragement or support to improve or leave the company. Everyone was suffering.

What is the impact if you do actively manage someone like Louise? She starts doing her job: she realises that someone is paying attention to her and, if it is handled well, she will feel that someone cares about her and her career. Beyond the immediate impact on Louise, her team also gets the manager they deserve. Colleagues who previously thought '*Why on earth do I work so hard, when she gets away with doing so little?*' see the change in her and feel that everyone is being held to the same standard – as a result, their motivation improves too. Everyone who is impacted by Louise's situation becomes more productive (even those self-driven, direct reports – imagine the amazing things they could achieve with a great manager). The company's customers are dealing with a motivated, informed, high-quality individual.

What is the situation if Louise doesn't improve, even after being given support and training? She needs to be managed out, and replaced with a hard-working individual who is keen to do their job and keep their skills up-to-date, while creating a great team.

Performance management can be hard and is usually viewed as dealing with negatives, but if handled in the right way, even those scenarios can involve a great deal of opportunity and positivity: an individual can become a high-performing credit to the company. The workplace becomes a much happier and more productive place, and the company's reputation as a positive environment to work within grows. Left unmanaged, one individual can have a hugely damaging effect across a team, department and sometimes a whole company.

The manager who has to hold multiple, difficult conversations with the individual concerned – and there will be more than one conversation – needs to invest a great deal of time and energy. They will be managing someone through what can be a long process with ups and downs, and the issue won't be resolved overnight. So, why do it? Putting aside the fact that it is your job, hopefully one of the reasons that you are a manager with responsibility for a team of any size is because you like people, and gain pleasure from seeing them develop and be motivated. You want them to enjoy their job and achieve success in their work. If you can guide someone from a low level of performance to high-achieving (or at least satisfactory, depending on their ability and what you can expect to achieve with that individual), your own sense of achievement will be boosted.

What if the individual doesn't improve: they don't respond, take you up on offers of training or support, or want to make a change? That is the point at which, sadly, they should go. But is it really sad? Not only is their departure better for the organisation, but also beneficial for them. Everybody should be happy in their work, and not every company is a good fit for an individual. If they leave and work elsewhere, they might thrive simply because their new firm is better suited to their personality or interests; it might even be an intangible quality that just feels right. No one should take this personally: we are all different, and we all belong in different places.

Often, showing your team members that you care about them is done by managing them and ensuring that they work to the standards you set. They need to know that you don't want to see them fail, get into trouble or gain a poor reputation, either in the company or beyond it. If no one shows Marcus or Louise that they care about their reputations, why should Marcus or Louise be concerned about them?

## Understand what motivates your team and colleagues

Why do your team members come to work each day? What makes them get out of bed of a morning? This is important to know, if you want to be able to manage them effectively and get the best out of them. It might be as simple as a need to pay the bills: that is fine, as long as they perform their role to an acceptable standard. At least you know not to constantly encourage them to go on training courses (other than the ones they are expected to attend as part of their role, of course), or apply for promotion. Apart from them not being interested, eventually you would irritate them and probably start to affect their performance. There is nothing wrong with the person who just wants to do their job and isn't focused on advancing.

Then there are the staff who are desperate to move up into management and are bored in their current role. For others, it might be pride in the company and its aims that get them excited every day. Michael Day, CEO, while I was working there, of Historic Royal Palaces, the UK charity that runs the Tower of London, Hampton Court Palace and other spectacular buildings, has an interesting take on motivation:

When managers talk about motivation, they often see it as a range of positive actions to motivate people who are otherwise neutral or poorly motivated. I've always believed that people are actually fundamentally well motivated. However, many organisations' and managers' approaches to the management of others is so poorly delivered that the individual becomes demotivated. So, people start off wanting to do a good job, being keen, wanting to progress, wanting to achieve, and then everything gets taken out of them by the systems, processes, culture, approaches to management, the poor behaviour of colleagues and managers.

It's not the failure of an individual to motivate you, it's a whole range of demotivating factors. A culture that isn't supportive, kind, generous and appreciative can eventually lead to your motivation going from way up 'here', to way down 'there'.

This makes sense. It's hard to imagine many people going into a new job actually wanting to fail or to be unhappy. Having an understanding of what motivates someone makes it easier for you to support and develop them – after all, you are supporting what already exists within them. Not only will you be helping them to gain greater pleasure during their time at work, but making it a whole lot easier for them to get out of bed in the morning – and let's face it, most of us could use a hand with that!

## Case Study

A training session was being run for a team of supervisors and their manager in an engineering firm – the subject on the agenda was motivation. They were all asked the question: 'On the days you are struggling with your job, what makes you get out of bed and go to work?' Everyone in the room enjoyed their job, but they all had quite specific interests and areas of work that excited them. The discussion led to an interesting revelation.

One of the supervisors, Hannah, had a problem with timekeeping: she was often late for meetings, or she would head out into the workshop area of the building and her colleagues wouldn't see her for hours.

Hannah's manager had spoken to her about it, and those conversations were increasingly formal. It turned out that she was always caught up in conversations with production workers, and would lose track of time. During the training session, when asked what got her out of bed in the morning, she said: 'I want our products to be perfect.' She went on to talk about how much she loved talking to other staff about the latest projects, and brainstorming improvements for products.

While it was wonderful to hear how much Hannah loved interacting with her colleagues and wanted their products to be the best in the business, she was also a supervisor and had dozens of other responsibilities for which she needed to be on time. However, instead of her lateness continuing to be an irritation, during the course of this 'what motivates you?' conversation, her colleagues and manager gained a greater level of understanding of her drive.

Hannah's manager now knew to ask about her interactions with her colleagues to get more insight into what she was learning each day. Hannah still had to improve her timekeeping, but at least everyone had a better handle on where she was and what she was doing. She was late because she was trying to do her absolute best for the customers and the company.

This knowledge meant that her manager would take a different approach when dealing with her timekeeping: he could take this information into account when considering the kind of projects to delegate to her, and it wasn't long before Hannah was seconded to a quality control project that really excited her. If an appropriate training event or conference came up, he could suggest it to her, and find work to inspire and motivate her at a deeper level. Hannah's colleagues also got a lot out of this training session, and vowed to find more informed ways of supporting her as she tried to tackle this problem.

Understanding what motivates each member of your team will help you understand behaviours, explain problems, provide opportunities, give you ways into conversations, and find ways to develop and support your staff.

Don't forget to share what drives *you* (although it is probably not a good idea to tell them if it is your pay cheque or fancy job title).

Your team members and colleagues will gain just as much from the information, and can encourage and support you too. After all, 'Followers want to be led by a person, not a role holder or a position filler or a bureaucrat'.[2] A shared understanding of motivations and interests can make the day job a whole lot more interesting for everyone, and stop you throwing your alarm clock across the room.

## Keeping appropriate distance from your team

Love your team? Great group of people? Fabulous – there is little better than working with a team whose company you enjoy. After a hard day at work you can all head to the pub together for a few drinks, you can stop being their manager for a few hours and let your hair down. Hold on a minute: *you are a manager.* You are *their* manager, and in order to do your job you need their respect. There needs to be a certain amount of distance, and over a drink at the pub, dinner or at a party is where so many managers make that mistake of crossing the line and getting too close to their team. This can be particularly challenging for those managers who have worked their way up within a company, and who are now managing those who are (or were) their friends.

---

[2] Rob Goffee and Gareth Jones (2015) *Why Should Anyone Be Led By You? What It Takes to Be an Authentic Leader,* p. 17.

> **Case Study**
>
> Sacha was a senior manager and good at his job. He would have been excellent but for one thing: the wider team found it difficult to respect him or take him too seriously. Often, he would join them in the pub and match them drink for drink. His team had seen him drunk, loud and undignified.
>
> Sacha was good company and a fun person to share a drink with, but the team now found it difficult to take him seriously if he was trying to discipline them or deal with other important issues – especially on the subject of 'appropriate conduct'.

It is unwise to get too close to your team on many levels. It can be challenging to deal with a problem, or to have others believe that you can be impartial, if those involved are your friends. If you want to pursue a career in management – especially if it involves working your way up in one company – there is no escaping the fact that this can have an impact on personal relationships, and you might have to adjust some of those dynamics. Some have found it a fairly smooth period of change, while others have found the transition hard.

Lynne, a health service manager in Sydney, Australia, talked to me about a colleague who found managing friends to be quite a challenge:

> She struggled to contain the conflicting needs of her team, couldn't say no easily, and ended up not having

enough staff on the occasions that she had granted all their leave requests. She then had to cover the jobs herself, essentially doing two jobs during staff leave and not getting much of anything done. She had to learn to leave her 'I will do everything to keep everyone happy' philosophy behind, and change it to: 'I can't please everyone and someone might not to be able to get the leave dates they want.'

It's certainly a challenge, and one that requires careful handling.

There is another downside to getting too close to your team. You need to be able to take an objective view of their strengths and weaknesses, and be in the best possible situation to support them and help them grow. Just like holding a book too close to your face, there is a point where everything becomes blurred and you are no longer able to see the picture clearly. Consider the following scenario.

## Scenario

Howard has a frontline management team of three reporting to him. He is extremely close to his managers and enjoys working with them. They are hard-working and more often than not, Howard works closely with them on their latest project or event and they have great fun. Their results are good, and he is extremely proud of all that they achieve. Although he is their manager, it feels more like a team of four than a team of three with him overseeing them.

During the course of a review meeting with his own director, Howard was asked what areas of work his team struggled with, or what he viewed as their areas of weakness. Howard thought for a while before replying that they didn't have any: they were an amazing team, and he couldn't think of anything they needed to work on. When asked if they needed any training or development he couldn't think of anything, as they were all so good at their jobs. Howard left the meeting pleased that he was able to talk so positively about his team.

The problem here is that Howard has not put the thought into anyone's minds that his team might want to progress, develop or get involved in organisation-wide projects, so they are not asked. As a result, the team is missing out on a number of great opportunities. His training budget, left unspent, is reduced each year. His team is not being stretched – and their skills and experience are not being grown. Howard has become so close to his team that he cannot see their weaknesses. They are a solid unit, but they will never move beyond that and, if anything, they might begin to stagnate and slip backwards.

In this scenario, there is irony in the fact that this great guy – who loves working with his team, and who supports and wants the best for them – has become the least equipped person to help them.

Whether as individuals or a collective, we all have strengths, weaknesses and areas in which we can improve. As a manager, you need to ensure that you can step back and reflect, to be able to assess the skills of your team objectively. A high-performing team is one that is always looking to improve.

Of course, none of this is to say that you shouldn't have a fun and enjoyable relationship with your team! By all means go for dinner with them after work, enjoy their company, but be careful and limit the amount of time that you are out with them. Perhaps you only go out for one drink or two. Maybe you just stay for the speeches or the birthday cake reveal at a party. Decide on a limit against which you can hold yourself accountable. It's best to avoid becoming involved with gossip – or to put it another way, talk *to* people, rather than *about* people.

## Tales over Coffee

I have never laughed as hard as I have with the team I managed at Hampton Court Palace in the south of England. The banter in the office was pretty constant, hilarious and unique. We knew quite a lot about one another's lives, we shared in each other's successes and were there to support each other if someone was going through a rough time.

The team was highly productive and I even joined them in the pub from time-to-time, but I was usually the first to leave. I was always their manager, and there was a line that we all recognised and respected.

## Under-promise, over-deliver

I love seeing enthusiastic, energetic, passionate managers who want to change the world – or at least be the best manager possible, bubbling with ideas to help their teams. However, it is worth keeping some of those ideas under your hat and surprising people with them. 'Under-promise, over-deliver' is a phrase you might have come across. It is useful in many aspects of your role, but when managing your team it will really pay off. Just scale back on what you publicly promise and make sure it is deliverable, then when you do get the job done, everyone will be happy. If you deliver even more than you promise, others will think you are amazing.

As a new and enthusiastic manager, it is often possible to overestimate what you can make happen in a period of time. All sorts of things can slow you down – so give yourself a break, and set up your team and colleagues for a nice surprise.

---

**Case Study**

Geoff worked in a big retail operation: he had taken over a large frontline team and their managers. He learned about under-promising and over-delivering early on in the job:

'Communication between those working on the floor and their managers was somewhere between poor and zero. I started the job determined to be a manager who would communicate well, often and honestly, and I wanted them to know what to expect.

---

So I drew up a communication plan, and presented it to the entire team over the course of a couple of briefings: how often 1-2-1s would take place, when I'd deliver briefings, team meetings, how often they would see their own managers, when annual appraisals would take place, the list went on. It was so long that each time I presented it to staff, I ran out of time! It was planned to within an inch of its life, and I was determined to implement it quickly.

The reality was that in the first year, I probably implemented about 30% of it. I now dread to think how my plans came across to the team during those briefings – probably like some overly detailed sergeant major. In the end I scrapped about 20% of it, and then it took about three years to get the remainder in place and increasingly seen as "business as usual". It was never going to happen overnight as I'd originally hoped.

I'm fortunate the team seemed to quickly forget my presentation, and never took the "but you promised" approach, which they could have so easily done. It was a hugely useful lesson for me – and I've learned to scale back what I publicly promise.'

Consider how much you reveal: play it carefully, and it will seem to others like you have superpowers (while saving yourself a lot of unnecessary stress).

## You need to be managed too

There is a particularly tricky people management challenge that you are bound to face along the way: *you*! You have a manager, right? If they are doing their job, then they should be proactively managing you in all the ways that you are managing your team, but perhaps less hands-on – after all, you are a manager with a job description that expects more self-direction, autonomy and decision making. The relationship with your own manager can make or break your experience in a job (just as your relationship with those who report into you can affect their experience of a role). Whatever the outcome, the responsibility for managing that relationship lies partly with you.

Your manager's job is to manage you: to monitor your work and give you feedback and constructive criticism – and let's not forget, if your attitude or performance is not up to scratch, they are paid to manage you back onto the right track, or out. Of course, they are also there to support, guide, develop and help you meet your career goals. Unfortunately, I have seen a lot of consistently excellent staff become difficult and defensive on the occasions that their manager rightly picks them up on something. No one is perfect, everyone makes mistakes: so if and when your turn comes, do take that feedback – encourage it, even – and use the experience as a learning opportunity.

Take the time to establish a positive and fruitful relationship with your manager: you can do plenty to make that happen. Admittedly, it can rest on your manager's capabilities and style, but you should do all that you can to lay the foundations. There will be times when you need to subtly manage them – what is known as 'managing upwards' (everyone needs that from time-to-time, even me!). In management, 'It's the person we follow, not the position'.[3]

Whether your manager is new (see Chapter 2) or has been in place for years but you have never really got to know them, try spending some time with them: go for a coffee. Find a slightly more relaxed setting than the office and get to know them a little better. Talk to them about their expectations of you, their preferred way of working and how you like to operate. Try and find out which of their buttons you don't want to press (for example, anyone who works for me should know that my big thing is deadlines: meet your deadlines or negotiate an extension, don't just miss them and come begging for forgiveness. Other than that, I am largely a pussycat!). It is also worth considering the following:

- Learn more about them and their responsibilities, the pressures they face and their workload.
- Do your research. Use LinkedIn and general Internet searches to learn more about them.
- Have they written articles, books?
- Is a video of a conference presentation they have made available online?

---

[3] Rob Goffee and Gareth Jones (2015) *Why Should Anyone Be Led By You? What It Takes to Be an Authentic Leader*, p. 205.

- What might their work history tell you about them?
- Chat to others about them, not in a 'dish the dirt' way, but merely 'Is there anything I should know?' (For example, if I heard that someone who was about to be managed by me was trying to learn more, depending on the way they approached it, I would think it very sensible.)

Be sure to schedule regular 1-2-1s with your manager: those meetings need to adapt to role, environment and needs, but it is important that they work for both of you, are focused and constructive, and that you have dedicated, undisturbed time together.

---

**Tales over Coffee**

Holding 1-2-1s with my previous managers has ranged from every two weeks (perhaps a bit over the top for the job and situation in question), monthly, every other month, and only when I put it in the calendar – and only then if he remembered to turn up.

The best scenario I found myself in was with a boss who scheduled to see me once a month. It didn't always happen but was agreed between us both, and we never went more than two months without a meeting. However, we had plenty of regular contact throughout the week as part of a positive, open and constructive relationship, so it really did work out fine.

Don't forget, this is *your* 1-2-1 – it's about *you*. I also would advise you always to turn up with potential solutions to any problems that you need to discuss with your manager. However, do bear in mind that they are not there to fix every issue you have, or to be a sounding board for general moaning. One senior manager I spoke to has lots of experience of junior managers going to him for advice because they are not getting on with their manager: 'This happens a lot. My advice is always to buy them a coffee and manage upwards. It always seems to help.'

Building a relationship with your manager is important. Sadly, this doesn't always happen: some people get stuck with managers who are challenging at best, and hellishly disruptive at worse. For those lucky enough to hit the jackpot, enjoy it but never forget that they are your manager – getting too close can be equally problematic.

I spoke to Jill, whose career includes an 18-month stint in a music organisation:

> My manager was an expert in his academic field, but he wasn't a skilled people manager. Distrusting of anything he didn't understand, you would struggle with him if your field wasn't his natural domain. He rarely said 'thank you', made no attempt to understand your management or learning style, or how he could get the best out of you. He seemed to have no interest in building any kind of real professional relationship. It was a classic case of a manager making or breaking your time in a role.

Once I learned that nothing would change and that my work and health would only suffer, I decided to leave.

Debbie, a team leader, talked about a manager who did very little work as far as she and her colleagues could tell: 'He had a knack for hiring talented people. We worked hard, did well and he got the kudos attached to that. Annoying, but on the flipside, he largely left us alone.'

Fortunately I have heard plenty of examples of great managers too, where the support goes both ways. Michelle is a teacher in Sydney, Australia:

> I'm currently supporting my own manager who has an ongoing conflict with another staff member. I'm there to listen when she needs to debrief, I attend mediation meetings as a support person. I've been offering advice in terms of industrial relations and workplace health and safety, both of which I have extensive knowledge of. Having me as a sounding board and offering practical options has been really successful.

### Tales over Coffee

The best manager I ever had is now a good friend. We had a wonderful, productive, enjoyable working relationship, but we both understood and respected who was in charge. I worked for him for six years and in that time we laughed a lot, achieved a

> huge amount, faced hurdles together, shared rants and frustrations, drank a lot of coffee and the occasional beer. He brought out the best in me, understood how I liked to work, and I understood how he operated.
>
> We achieved this pretty quickly too, because we were both open to talking things through and having an honest, transparent relationship. We also both enjoyed what we did and wanted to keep on enjoying it, so we were purposeful about supporting each other, even when we faced challenges.

A positive relationship with your line manager is priceless. Understand one another's roles, play your part in making that relationship work (even if you have to do some of the 'driving'), take them plenty of solutions, and buy them the occasional coffee. You will make your own life easier, while doing the same for them.

People are the lifeblood of any organisation's work: they have the ideas and deliver the final product. They shape your company's reputation. Whether you have a team of one or 101, the chances are that the work you produce with them will become some of your greatest achievements and proudest moments – but it is down to you to provide the framework for that to happen.

Try and understand the reasons for people's behaviour, learn what motivates them, and put in place clear standards to which you expect them to work. However, none of this operates in a vacuum. Running alongside this is the need for a positive, supportive, creative culture – and this is where you come into the picture.

# 2
# Culture

## Introduction

In the last few years of my career I have really come to appreciate the importance and impact of workplace culture. We spend more time at work than at home, and more time with our colleagues than our family – so it's hugely important that we want to be there.

As a manager, this translates into ensuring your team members are operating within an environment that helps them feel welcome, valued, empowered and, hopefully, happy to be there. A lot of frontline teams work schedules with unusual hours: evenings, weekends and public holidays, in which case you might need to give this even more thought; your team has to work when everyone else is relaxing, celebrating or spending time with their friends and families.

But culture isn't just about whether or not this is a fun place to work; it is also about standards and expectations, what sort of work ethic and quality of work is considered the norm. For example:

- How do people treat each other?
- How do you resolve problems?
- Does everyone feel valued, that they are making a worthwhile contribution?
- What sort of style and approach does your team as a collective possess, and have become known for?

The grand task of making an individual happy is largely out of your hands (more on that later), but you can have a huge impact on the culture in which they operate. You can't just make it all up, though – you are not (or shouldn't be) working in a silo.

Michael Day explains:

> There's a responsibility for the manager to understand what the prevailing organisational culture is. It's massively important that they're working within the culture that the whole organisation has established, or is seeking to establish; otherwise, if you try to start something different, it becomes very uncomfortable – either for you or your team, or both.

So often I hear managers complain about disruptive staff, negativity, how other teams don't give them the respect they deserve. After I chat with them for just a short while, I sometimes discover that they are their own problem. It really is as simple as this: if you let people get away with poor behaviour or attitude, then you have set the standard – low. Consider this scenario.

**Scenario**

A manager feels that their staff do not receive the respect they deserve. Other departments don't communicate well with them, and are reluctant to engage on projects. The manager is frustrated, angry and feels marginalised. However, if the manager were to look inside their own team, rather than assume that the problem lies elsewhere, they might find that the issue lies a little closer to home.

Perhaps the team don't get on with each other, or they don't communicate well with each other, so other departments are always getting mixed messages. Perhaps a negative, unsupportive culture is such that other departments don't want to be around them.

We can take this a step further and ask: who is responsible for ensuring that a negative culture doesn't develop? Who should be setting standards and ensuring the team meets those standards? As the manager of the team, it is their responsibility to set standards, communicate them clearly, monitor the team's performance and respond appropriately when things aren't going well.

Here, the issues that the manager is experiencing with other departments are actually of their own making.

Ask yourself:

- What is it that you want for your team, and for yourself?
- What are your personal ideals, those of your fellow managers and your organisation?

They are all part of the mix, and usually can be broken down into fairly simple concepts:

- To be the best you possibly can
- To go home each day knowing that you did the best you could
- To be a team known for fixing problems, not creating them
- To be a team known for being friendly and approachable.

The list goes on, and it is not rocket science. But as the manager, you are responsible for taking action whenever standards drop below those that you, the team and the company have set.

Unless you aspire to a 'clock-in, clock-out' culture, then you have a tough, ongoing job on your hands. But a team that is growing and learning, challenging itself, achieving great things, holding itself to high standards and hopefully having a blast at the same time, is an amazing thing. As mentioned in Chapter 1, you will have bad days as well as good, but you will learn from those. If you get the culture of your team right, there will be no limits to what you can all achieve.

## Making your team happy

What about just plain ol' having fun and being happy in the workplace? To what extent is it your job to invest in the team's happiness? So long as they do their job, are not miserable and the work isn't doing them harm physically, mentally or emotionally, surely they should not really expect any more of you? After all, we choose our own mood and state of mind.

By now you can probably guess that this is not my approach. I believe that we do have some responsibility to try and create an environment and culture where people can be happy at work. They might still welcome a lottery win and the chance to walk away from it all, but while they have to work, it should be as enjoyable as possible.

There are plenty of reports and statistics on how being happy at work makes you more productive and creative. Among these is a 2017 report by researchers at the University of Bristol in the UK, who found that productivity in happy employees increased by 10%.[4] Research from the Social Market Foundation put it at 12%.[5]

---

[4] Eugenio Proto (2016) 'Are happy workers more productive?', IZA World of Labor.
[5] Daniel Sgroi (2015) 'Happiness and productivity: Understanding the happy-productive worker', Social Market Foundation.

## Tales over Coffee

I will be honest, I am not a statistics person: a page full of figures doesn't do much for me. I would rather base things on experience – mine and that of others – discussed, of course, over the obligatory coffee!

Statistics aside, you will get a lot more out of me if I am enjoying my work, the company of my colleagues, the environment. You will get better ideas out of me if I can laugh and banter, knock ideas around uninhibited, and get distracted by the earworm tune of the day or the latest silly meme to land in my inbox.

Even when writing this book, I was much more productive surrounded by the noise of a cafe, stopping every now and again to message a friend and share my thoughts, or ask a question. I also know that the teams I have managed have performed better when they were able to be themselves, had fun and an emotional connection to one another and their work.

As a manager, it is indeed your job to invest in your team's happiness: to create an environment where people can flourish and feel valued. If they choose not to engage then that is up to them, but at least you will have fulfilled your part of the deal. It is also your job to get to know your direct reports, understand how to get the best out of them and – within limits, of course – put those things in place. Some practices to build into your own ways of working and that of your team are:

- Creating clear routes for communication – making sure that you listen and respond, showing that you value their opinion (see Chapter 3)
- Investing in training and development (see Chapters 4 and 5)
- Celebrating successes, and supporting one another when things don't go to plan
- Putting in place opportunities to enjoy one another's company in a relaxed environment
- Getting to know your team members, their strengths and weaknesses
- Giving newcomers a warm welcome (see the next section)
- Putting in place clear boundaries and tackling problems.

It is unlikely that you will be in a position to have any influence over salary or benefits, so do focus on the things on which you can have an impact.

Whatever the output of your organisation, your business is fundamentally *people*. They are your most valuable assets: 'staff, not stuff'. If your staff are happy and productive, the 'stuff' will naturally follow.

What of the individual's responsibility? Without intending to sound like the quote of the day on a box of lentils, we are all are responsible for finding our own happiness. Everybody – managers and team members alike – should be seeking out the training and development to ensure they have the skills to do their jobs well, thus adding to the enjoyment factor. Everybody should be tackling problems and having those difficult conversations, so they are not hanging over them like a dark cloud and ruining their day. Everybody should be having fun, not forgetting that all work and no play makes Jack a dull boy (or girl).

As a manager you don't have control over a team member's attitude: only they can choose whether to come to work with a positive mindset, or walk through the door like a big grey rain cloud and proceed to rain on your collective parade. There are limits to a manager's superpowers, but you can do your bit and lead by example – even if that is just taking your sense of humour into work with you each day.

Reflect on your own attitude. Are you going into work in a positive frame of mind, and building on that in the company of your colleagues? What if it turns out that, on reflection, you are a negative influence? If you really cannot do any more to improve your lot, if you really are unhappy and can't find the joy or motivation: try as you might you can't build a positive relationship with your colleagues or manager, then perhaps it is time for you (or your team member, if this is about them) to find your happiness elsewhere. Mainly for your own sake, but possibly also for the sake of your colleagues and the business (see the case study about 'Louise' in Chapter 1).

However, this should not be read as failure. As I outlined in Chapter 1, some jobs simply are not a good fit for us, and it is incredibly positive if you can recognise that and make the appropriate move. Life is not a dress rehearsal, we don't get a second chance at this – so make sure you are happy, and contributing to the happiness of those around you.

## Tales over Coffee

I had my own 'lightbulb moment' many years ago. In the early days of taking on a large team and managing them through a big period of change, I was trying all sorts of things to get them on-side.

As you can imagine – and as is the norm with any change curve – some were coming with me, while others were not. Some resisted for good reason, some out of sheer bullheadedness. I was working to improve things for the business, but a large part of that was also about improving the team's working circumstances. I wanted them to be happy and fulfilled in their work, to have all the tools they needed. No matter what I did, there were always some that kicked back.

At this time I cycled to and from work each day, a wonderful hour in each direction when I could prepare for the day ahead, or work through the issues of the day before I got home. I often talked out loud, and on the bike it was no different (no doubt free entertainment for the pedestrians I passed!).

I distinctly remember cycling home one evening, trying to figure out how I could make them all happy, every one of them. What was I missing? What would work on certain individuals I just couldn't seem to win round? I was desperate to do my best for them and make them all, well, happy. Then it hit me:

*I can't. No matter how hard I try, I cannot make them all happy. I'll just drive myself crazy trying.*

I was doing everything I could to create an environment in which, if they chose to engage, they could have a positive, fulfilling experience and even some fun. The next bit – the choosing to be happy bit – well, that was in their hands.

As any change model will show you, there will always be those who will not get on board, so don't spend your time and energy on those who won't budge. Instead, invest in those who have, or who will over time. *You cannot make everyone happy.*

## Welcoming new team members

'First impressions count', is a rather tired and obvious adage, but one of which not enough recruiters take note. If you manage people, at some point you will become a recruiter. If you are responsible for a large team, you probably recruit more often than you would like. Unfortunately, being a busy frontline manager doesn't leave you much time to dedicate to this, but it is important that you find that time. A swift, ill-judged, so-called 'welcome' can lead to people leaving quicker than you would like, then you just have to recruit all over again. So, save yourself some time (and the company some money), and give new team members a proper welcome the first time round.

A lot of books and websites talk about the questions you should ask at interview, the challenges and exercises you should put the candidates through as part of an assessment, and which are the best psychometric tests to use. Often, they stop there, and the next step in the process is neglected. What kind of welcome are you giving them once you have offered them the job?

When you have appointed them, you can write a letter telling them how much you are looking forward to them joining you. Next steps:

- Put together their training programme and send it to them in advance, so they know what to expect.
- Assign them a buddy, and ask them to drop the new starter an email to say hello.
- If they are management or have an office-based role, make sure their calendar has been populated with important meetings and welcome coffees with new colleagues.
- Put time aside for them to get to know their team members.
- If they have to wear a uniform, make sure you have their measurements, collected their new clothes and assigned them a locker.

All of this will make them feel welcome, wanted and appreciated. The impression you make starts before their interview, continues through that process, and doesn't stop when they are offered the job. Starting a new job is tough – how you welcome your recruits says a lot about you as a manager, and can set the tone for your relationship with your new hire.

Before I continue, I just want to remind you to do something else after the interviews. Do give feedback to the unsuccessful candidates – assuming, of course, that they want it. I have always believed that anyone who makes it to interview deserves feedback (internal and external candidates alike). If the candidate is internal and did not make it to interview, they should be entitled to feedback on their written application too – after all, this is a part of their development.

The whole process of applying for a job, even if you don't get it, is a hugely important and informative process. If you want to support and develop your team (or anyone from within your company), it is essential to invest time in giving them feedback and letting them know what they need to do to stand a better chance next time.

---

**Tales over Coffee**

I once had a team member who applied for the same management job three times – she was successful on her third attempt. I took the time to talk with her about her performance on each occasion, and she listened and took action.

It was a long hard road for her, but she chose to adopt a positive attitude, learned a great deal, and is now a superb manager.

---

As I mentioned at the beginning of this chapter, frontline managers often find themselves with something extra to factor in when planning training and the welcome their staff will receive: weekend working. It is not uncommon for frontline managers – especially those who oversee public-facing teams – to have staff who work weekends. If new recruits are only contracted to work weekends and are unavailable on weekdays, you can find yourself with a problem if trainers from other departments work only Monday to Friday and are unwilling to make exceptions.

The challenge of getting non-operational departments to take into account the needs of teams who work seven days a week is worthy of a whole book in itself (and outside the scope of this one), but I do understand your frustration. If you have attempted to do battle over this but got nowhere, a different approach is required. Try and view it as a development opportunity for some of your other team members, and get them trained up during the week so that they can train colleagues at the weekend. Not only are your new weekend staff now up-to-speed, but you also have some team members who have just boosted their CV (resumé), been shown how much you trust them, and can help in other projects down the road – as they are now part of your very own training team.

The issue of a proper welcome applies across the board, regardless of the new arrival's level of seniority. If perhaps you think this is a problem only for those lower down the staffing structure, and senior managers are welcomed with grand lunches and desk drawers full of stationery, think again!

**Case Study**

Tina had been appointed to a senior position in a university department.

'I knew that I had inherited a challenging team, and there were a lot of problems I needed to tackle, which was fine – it's what I do, and I like a challenge. Before I even arrived for my first day, the HR manager would contact me and talk about my "poisoned chalice", my "teams from hell", how certain teams I would be managing were "a nightmare". He would talk unfavourably about particular managers who would be reporting to me.

Apart from making me feel like I was walking into a job with absolutely no redeeming features, it had another awful effect which I only realised after I'd been doing the job for a year: these managers stood absolutely no chance with me. They weren't allowed a first impression or to build their own relationship with me. No matter how hard I tried, I had been unduly influenced by the overpowering negativity that had been communicated to me before I arrived.

The arrival itself? The director of the organisation (and my boss) had forgotten I was coming, and had to be reminded the day before. My office was a mess, paint peeling off the walls; dirty, out-of-date notices falling off tatty noticeboards. My computer took a couple of days to set up, and I had to buy my own printer a couple of weeks in, as one hadn't been provided and no one was interested in helping me source one. No one had sourced any stationery for me. I had no formal induction or training plan, and no meetings had been set up for me. On a couple of occasions I was asked why I hadn't attended certain meetings – it was because I had no idea they even existed, let alone known I was meant to attend!

Of course, everyone blamed everyone else. HR blamed those who now worked for me, and they blamed HR. My new manager, the director, had done nothing, despite having a PA who could have done much of it for him, had he asked. It was an unwelcoming, negative, lonely, so-called "welcome".

It set the tone for my time there, and I left 12 months later.'

## Welcoming your new manager

It is very possible that you won't just be welcoming new team members. At some point in your career you are bound to be welcoming a new manager too – *your* manager – and that is a welcome for which you also carry some responsibility.

## Case Study

Pam is based on the East Coast of the USA. She had not been in her sales job all that long before she got a new, West Coast-based manager. He seemed a nice enough guy, but he very quickly began to ask her to make changes to the way that she did things. He also wanted to fly over and spend three weeks travelling and attending appointments with her.

Pam was immediately resentful: she was used to working on her own, and had no idea what he wanted to get out of the visit. She was becoming stressed and frustrated. Eventually she let off steam to a colleague, who made a number of points for Pam to consider:

- You need to do your bit to build a positive relationship with him, so try not to go into this from a place of negativity.
- He's new, and he's trying to find his feet in a new company. He might be a senior manager, but he is also human – give the guy a chance.
- You have no idea what targets or objectives he has been given by his own manager – this might not be coming from him.

In this situation, Pam might have to direct things a little more. For example, by insisting on a meeting before she starts attending the appointments with him, so she can be clear on the reasons for this trip. If he is assessing her performance, how is he going to measure her success?

Pam needs to plan how they are going to carry out the visits, who is going to lead the conversation. Is he only there to observe her? To be fair, he should be leading on all of this, but he is not – so Pam might need to step up and do it.

It is important to remember that your manager's job is to observe you at work and assess your performance. Do listen to their feedback: they might also offer you some really useful training or further development, as we all have areas in which we can improve.

A key thing to remember when a new manager arrives and you find aspects of their arrival difficult: they are new, and they are human! Everyone needs time to adapt to a new job – even extremely senior staff should receive an induction and be given the time and support to learn and adapt. Some cope with this period better than others, while some come in like a steamroller and get it all wrong very quickly.

Equally, despite doing all that you can to make things easier and pave the way for a positive relationship, you may still find you have a boss who makes your cat look like a genius – but at least you know you tried!

Whether or not your company has a formal on-boarding or induction programme, you should be part of that process. Make your new manager feel welcome, and win yourself some brownie points at the same time:

- Prepare a pack for them to have on their arrival.
- Include a summary of the team's current projects and your priorities.
- Include the names and photos of your team members, to give them a head start on getting to know people.
- Put a coffee in their calendar and get to know them. Fill them in (constructively) on the current state of play in your team, but don't offload your problems onto them straightaway.

Your new manager will be able to engage thoroughly in the conversation, as they will have read the pack you so thoughtfully created. This way you will have a manager who is up-to-speed quickly – which is advantageous for you – and they will see that they have an organised and thoughtful manager on their team. It's a win-win!

You can have a huge amount of fun welcoming people into your team, and your current team members should be involved, their own relationships benefiting in the process. You can review and refresh what is important to you about your team's culture, and ensure that new staff are getting the message you want them to hear. This is also a great opportunity to ensure that they are in the best possible position to make an enthusiastic, productive start to their time in the company. They will be happier, be up-to-speed and on the same wavelength as their colleagues much quicker – all of which makes your life a whole lot easier.

## Always do the right thing

You are a good person. Your instinct is to do the right thing, regardless of whether or not anyone will ever know, or whether you could get away with doing nothing. Once you are in a position of increased responsibility, there is no escaping the fact that you now lead by example – no matter how tough it gets, or the myriad of genuine, reasonable excuses you could have to hand.

If you do the wrong thing or cut corners, people will know – and surely that is not something for which you want to be known. Your reputation also rubs off on your management team colleagues and team members. You might even find yourself being bypassed because colleagues want to talk to your nicer, better peers.

I will talk about this in more detail in the next section, but suffice to say: if you make a mistake, fix it. Sometimes you can do it quickly and discreetly, and no one need be any the wiser. If that is not possible or appropriate (and that is a lot of the time), it is best simply to hold your hands up and take the hit. Honesty is something that everyone appreciates.

---

**Tales over Coffee**

A couple of years ago I started a new job in which I was responsible for a large department with a number of teams. One morning I stood before the largest of the teams to introduce myself. I told them about my background and a little of my career to date. I finished my briefing with:

'I can only make one promise to you, one guarantee: I will make mistakes. I'm human, and I'm bound to get it wrong on occasions. If I realise I will say so, and apologise. If I don't realise, tell me. Let me know if I get it wrong or upset you. We can talk about it and I can work on getting it right. Does that sound fair?'

There were a lot of nodding heads and positive murmuring. I got some great feedback, and started my relationship with that team on a very positive footing. You cannot just say it, though – you have just set a standard against which you will be measured.

Your team is like a room full of elephants – they will never forget!

---

Your next task? Making sure that your team takes the same approach. That is a tough one, but not impossible. As mentioned previously, leading by example means letting them know what is expected, and talking to them when they are not meeting the standards set.

Coping with other people's poor behaviour or low standards – and the temptation to meet them at their level – is another thorny issue to tackle. No matter what happens or how badly people behave, it is important to try and 'be better than that'. This is in no way about striving to be liked by everyone – that is impossible and will lead you down all sorts of unsuccessful routes (if your main aim in life is to be liked, don't become a manager!). This is about maintaining your cool, being professional, supportive, a team player: no matter what is thrown your way, you never throw it back because you are better than that.

This is a hard one to learn, and tough to carry through in the heat of the moment. It's one of those topics I have had to discuss many times with frustrated managers who have yet to engage in muck-flinging or to put the stops on helping someone, no matter how badly they have wanted to do so. I reminded them: 'You are better than that, be the better person.' Once you have cracked that, work to create a culture that ensures your team as a whole takes that approach as well. However, this can be challenging if other teams in the company do not work to the same standards as you. For example:

'Finance managers never finish their staff reviews on time, so why should we?'

'Maintenance don't manage staff who turn up late, so why should we?'

'The catering team aren't made to wear name badges, so why should we?'

The answer? 'Because we are better than that.'

In no way should this take a negative or competitive tone: it's 'better than *that*', rather than 'better than *them*'. It is really important to set your own standards high, meet them, then support your team to meet them too.

## It's OK to make mistakes

On those occasions when you have dropped the ball, confess! Either ask for help, or accept the help offered to you. Raise the issue with your manager first, or if they raise it with you and you know you are in the wrong, say so (never let your manager find out from another source – even if they are not annoyed by your mistake, they will be annoyed that they were taken unawares and found out from a third party). Apologise, take the feedback: learn from it, and you can both move on. If you don't, it might become a long, drawn-out and painful problem.

In fact, it is not impossible for the end result to be along the lines of this scenario.

**Scenario**

Jess has worked very hard to get a job in a company she loves. She is ambitious, enthusiastic and keen for more responsibility. After a while her manager hands her an important, challenging project, and makes it clear that she is there to support Jess throughout.

As the project progresses, Jess starts to experience problems but she is unwilling to admit that she needs help. Mistakes start to be made, but when she is asked for updates, Jess insists that all is well. Eventually, not only her work but her attitude begins to deteriorate. Jess is called into a meeting with her manager, who has concerns. Jess becomes defensive and won't say anything other than 'Everything is fine'. The problems continue, and Jess still fails to ask for help or acknowledge that she is making mistakes.

The next meeting to take place now involves both her manager and a representative from human resources. Again, Jess refuses to admit that anything is wrong: when presented with evidence of her mistakes, she declines to talk.

Knowing that her job is on the line, Jess resigns and leaves the company with a poor reputation.

This might sound far-fetched, but it can happen very easily. Why would Jess not admit that she needed help? There are many potential reasons: perhaps she didn't want to reveal what she felt was a weakness, perhaps she was proud or afraid. It might be that in her previous jobs, mistakes were not considered acceptable and would have got her into a great deal of trouble. Maybe she did not want to admit to having bitten off more than she could chew. Whatever the reason, a situation like this is incredibly sad. If Jess had asked for help when she was struggling, acknowledged her mistakes and engaged in an honest conversation, she would have been credited as someone who wanted to learn, knew when to apologise and when to ask for input.

It is one thing to know that it is OK to make mistakes, but we still curse ourselves when we get things wrong. One of my managers used to say that if I got something wrong, he would not have to do much more than acknowledge it, because I would punish myself more than he ever could – and he was right. I know I am not alone in this, so when we find it so hard to allow ourselves to fail, how on earth can we help others to see that it is OK?

Building a culture where people want to be their absolute best and strive for it, but also where it is OK when things don't go to plan, is key. In messing something up, you are simply showing yourself to be human and experiencing an important part of the learning process. Moreover, while we are all familiar with the concept of learning by our mistakes, and we all know it to be true, it's also helpful to learn from other people's errors. So, help your team learn and admit when you get it wrong, instead of trying to find excuses. When you are honest with your team, you will gain trust and respect from them, as they see that you are unlikely to hide things.

David Hingley, Chief Operating Officer for The Landmark Trust, certainly doesn't see apologising as a weakness: 'Apologising for a mistake isn't weak – the best managers I've worked with are the ones who do just that. They make it a strength.'

When a team member makes a mistake, depending on the nature of the error, they might just need to learn from it and move on. However, sometimes an employee's actions can have serious consequences – in which case you still need to have a no-nonsense conversation with them, but in a helpful, productive way:

- Get them to talk through what has happened, step-by-step.
- Help them understand – and possibly clarify for yourself – where they went wrong.
- Find out what you could have done differently to support them.
- See if they need further training or resources.

Make sure they understand that you are there to help ensure they don't make the same mistake again. Be sure they fully understand where they went wrong, and can outline very clearly to you what they will do differently next time. Get them to do the talking and tell you: this is a good way of ensuring that they really do understand, and are clear on their next steps, rather than just nodding as you do the talking. Present the situation in terms of what 'we' can do to stop 'this' happening again: reassure them that they are not alone; you are a team, and you have an important part to play in helping them to move forward as their manager.

Fear of failure can stifle creativity, and put people off having a go at all. Your team will never shine if everyone is too afraid of dropping the ball even to pick it up in the first place. Mistakes are impossible to avoid, so embrace them and make them a part of how you work. Don't aim to never make another mistake; instead, aim to make better mistakes tomorrow.

## Being nice isn't a weakness

How nice are you? Silly question? Not so much in some businesses. In some quarters, being nice is seen as a weakness, and people feel they have to be cutthroat in order to get what they want – but we really don't. For example, some of the nicest people I know are some of the most senior people around. They have climbed to the top in some very challenging industries, and wield a lot of power and influence. You probably wouldn't want to mess with them, but if you were to, they would respond in a wholly professional manner – and wouldn't go on to trash your career.

How you behave on your way up the career ladder – how you behave in general – can make or break you. Your reputation will stick with you, and if it is not positive you might find yourself spending a lot of your precious energy trying to rectify it. Put simply: people will talk. Your reputation follows you – and in some cases, arrives before you. It can cross departments, organisations and even entire countries (the Phileas Fogg of industry gossip!). Your reputation is a hardy traveller, a fine adventurer worthy of membership of the National Geographic Society. Doubt its stamina and tenacity at your peril.

A negative reputation can shape the culture of your whole team, and you will struggle to achieve things if colleagues or external stakeholders do all they can to avoid you, or have the least amount of contact possible. Get a reputation for being a nice group of people to do business and spend time with, and they will be hammering at your door.

Actively seek opportunities to be nice: for example, tell someone how useful their contribution to a meeting was; in this age of digital communication, tell someone when you see that they have beautiful handwriting, or compliment their tie. However, do be careful not to make your compliments too personal – there is a great deal of sensitivity around sexual harassment in the workplace, and ill-judged compliments can veer into this area. Don't let this stop you saying anything, just get to know your colleagues, give it a bit of thought and you will be fine – your workplace will be all the nicer for it. The outcome? Not only will you make your colleagues feel good, but you will feel pretty good too.

Oddly, some people feel the need to have permission to say this kind of thing: after all, it's a personal comment, especially if the workplace is pretty austere. So, set the tone in your team. Most importantly, make sure that anything you say is genuine – otherwise your team will see right through you, and the impact will be worse than saying nothing at all.

## The importance of saying 'thank you'

It astounds me that people still need reminding of the importance of two powerful little words that can transform the workplace: 'Thank you.'

Many people are fortunate enough to work in an environment where saying 'thank you' is a regular part of the daily lexicon; however, there are still too many people who don't. I have personal experience of both ends of the spectrum, and the extent to which my colleagues and I felt appreciated had an enormous impact on our work life – and, no doubt, the overall performance of our departments.

There is a lot of talk about reward and recognition schemes within organisations. The form of recognition that gets the most positive outcomes is not big awards or financial bonuses, bottles of wine or free weekends away. The biggest impact on the workplace comes from a general and powerful culture of appreciation, where people say 'thank you' to one another, and make it clear how much they value others and their efforts.

We don't need a raft of statistics to tell us that a happy and appreciated team of people is going to be more productive, dedicated and engaged (although there are examples in the 'Making your team happy' section above). But even if it doesn't increase productivity, doesn't everyone want their staff to be happy? As for those managers who are not really bothered so long as output is high, do you really want to work for people like that?

It is not just about top-down recognition either: showing gratitude to your own managers, acknowledging the support or opportunities they have given you, is just as relevant. Then there are your colleagues: when did you last compliment a colleague on a job well done, even if you were not involved with their project? It's so important to look out for opportunities to say 'well done'. As well as making the individual feel valued, it contributes to an overall culture that benefits everyone concerned. If you are a manager, your role is to set the tone and define the culture: another case of leading by example, one with which you can have a lot of fun, and from which you can gain a lot of pleasure.

Saying 'thank you' isn't difficult or expensive – in fact, the simplest, personal methods are often the best. In an age when everything is electronic, a handwritten note is always warmly received, or why not take someone out for a coffee? Just dedicating an hour of your time to someone makes a big statement.

**Tales over Coffee**

I keep a stash of thank-you cards in my office drawer at the ready, and I always enjoy an opportunity to write a personalised note to let someone know what a difference they have made to me.

Making the note personal and not just 'thanks very much' is key: showing that you acknowledge them, the individual, that you truly recognise what they have done and the impact it has had.

That stash of cards? Most of the time (I confess to the occasional blip) they too are personalised, I have had them made with photos I have taken, or ordered custom stationery. I have always put thought into it, as I don't want anyone to feel like I have dashed off generic messages, and the card could be for almost anyone.

These are all nice things for me to do for others, but the pleasure I get out of doing it means I benefit too. It's a win-win!

What about those who don't seem to need thanks or acknowledgement to drive them, for whom it is simply about getting the job done? That is OK too, as not everyone feels they need it. However, failing to show them gratitude makes you remiss as a colleague or manager: after all, what you are doing is displaying good manners as well as positive, supportive workplace behaviour, so why would you not? There is something else to look out for, especially if an individual is in a managerial role: are they showing appreciation to their team? Are they encouraging a positive, supportive culture? Are they leading by example, regardless of their own personality type and needs?

So simple, and yet so rarely covered on management training courses. Why isn't one of the first things we are taught as new managers the importance and benefits of saying 'thank you', or the need to create a work environment where our team members do the same? One would think people wouldn't need to be told this, but personal experience tells me otherwise.

Some points to consider:

- Your thanks should be timely.
- They must be genuine.
- They don't need to have monetary value, but try and make them personal and specific to that person.
- Make sure your colleagues, leaders and the people you work with from other organisations receive appropriate thanks and feel valued too.
- If you are impressed by someone's performance, don't just let them know – tell their manager too.

It doesn't take much to create a happy, valued, productive and creative team of people. All it will cost you is two heartfelt little words. I guarantee there is someone deserving of a note from you right now – so what are you waiting for?

## Recognising 'invisible' team members

How's your backbone? No, I'm not questioning your moral fibre! Most large teams have 'backbones'. You know the type: they turn up on time, are always dressed appropriately or in uniform, and rarely cause you any problems. They will not be the first to sign up for overtime, and in some cases they will not do any at all. They don't get involved in projects and they are not interested in career development. They clock in and clock out without any fuss, and get on with the job they are paid to do. You often forget they are there because they are so reliable, and anyway you are busy with the troublesome ones; while the 'shining stars' who are doing you proud, sign up for every project and have a great future ahead of them, are also taking up quite a lot of your time.

You might think of your backbone as a bit dull, uninspired even: not interested in pushing themselves or drawing attention to themselves – but don't ever underestimate their importance to the success of your team. You never have to pull them up for anything because they are doing what the company asks of them, freeing up your time to deal with those who are being difficult and presenting you with challenges. Without your backbone you could not do all the development work with others.

Who is it that willingly moves to another post or task, or changes their break so your rising star can go off and attend a meeting or go to a training session?
Who keeps the day-to-day activities running while special events take place?

If every member of your team wanted to be the next manager or progress in some other way, how would you cope? You don't have the resources or time to support everyone in this way. Moreover, you would have to spend a huge amount of your time recruiting, because there would always be someone leaving to climb up the next rung of the career ladder. However, your backbone will always be there, on time, looking smart and giving a good, solid performance.

The problem here is that because they are so solid, and your attention is being drawn by others, backbones are often forgotten. They are invisible, which means that you are less likely to remember to thank them. Because their work isn't standout amazing, the chances are that you are less likely to reward their performance. They will not be associated with the latest hot project, so they are not the first people who come to mind when awards are handed out, or when staff receive special mentions in briefings or newsletters.

If this is the case in your team, their colleagues need to see how central backbones are to their ability to go and do things – and they need to learn to show their appreciation. In turn, you need to make sure they realise how grateful you are too. Even the backbones themselves might not realise what a critical role they play, and this has to change.

Start watching the steady ones who normally pass under your radar, and make sure they feel like the backbone of your team – because that is what they are.

## The essential role of disruptors

I guarantee you have disruptors in your team. No matter what you say or do, there they are, questioning you. Your explanations are never enough, even for the smallest, simplest change. It will be the same couple of people, and your heart will sink as you see them raise their hand in a briefing, or as they appear at your office door just after you have announced a new policy or procedure. You might feel like they are never happy, always doubting you and your decisions. But turn this situation on its head and they can be hugely beneficial to your work, as well as an important part of your team's success: as crazy as this might sound, you should welcome them.

Having someone (appropriately and professionally) question your ideas and actions can help you clarify things in your own mind. They might have spotted a hole you have missed, or bring you an idea that takes your plans an exciting step further. Engaging them in useful conversation, and asking them for constructive feedback (rather than moaning for the sake of it), gives you further opportunity to explore your aims with them.

Of course, there are those who are simply out to wind up the boss. But once they realise that you are not going to get annoyed and that they are failing to 'push your buttons', they will give up and go away. If it sinks in that you are going to ask questions of them and expect them to think – that you are open to dialogue and, in fact, encourage it – the ones who are doing it just for the sake of being difficult will start to back down. Those that stick around a little longer and persist with their unconstructive approach might require a conversation about their aims and their own reputation as a vessel of negativity.

However, the real disruptors will push you and encourage you to think harder and deeper. They are curious, they want clarity and understanding, and for things to be as successful as possible. They have something to contribute and are essential for a lively, productive team that is always pushing the boundaries. Channel their energy and curiosity, and soon you will be able to distinguish between those who are genuinely seeking the best possible outcome, and those who have nothing better to do than waste your time.

Make the most of those disruptors. When they appear at your door, give them the shock of their life – invite them in for a coffee and welcome their questions.

## Getting your team to manage one another

As a manager, you are not the only one who can define and lead a positive culture within your team. It can be incredibly successful when it comes from *inside* the team. People are more likely to stick within boundaries that they have helped define, and new staff will find it easier to navigate their way into a culture when everyone around them has had a part to play in its development.

**Tales over Coffee**

This was done with great success when I was at Hampton Court Palace, and the final result was a charter, 'The Way We Talk', which became the benchmark for standards of behaviour in the team.

The charter was created at a time when the relationship between the management team and team members was strained and, significantly, every team member and manager contributed to the process of developing it. It resulted in a number of standards that made clear the expected behaviour and quality of communication that occurred between everyone – whether between team members and managers, team member to team member or manager to manager.

Over time, the charter became a way of peers managing peers as they held one another to account, and eventually the language used within it was subsumed into our daily language. As managers, we also found it an incredibly useful way to recognise those who were performing to a high standard, not just those who were underperforming.

Bring your whole team together, either in one go or in groups, and invite everyone to pool their ideas and define the standards of work, how you treat each other and how you communicate. You may be surprised by what you can achieve after just a few meetings and piles of sticky notes. But *everyone* must be held accountable, and the standards should be built into your daily work life and more formal processes, such as your annual reviews. Try and ensure that these are embedded into all aspects of your team's work life.

Steve Sargeant, an experienced customer services manager, has seen this work:

> Our team worked together to come up with a list of values. We referred to them every day, and they informed the kind of culture we wanted to encourage. We put them at the heart of all our training, and they were increasingly at the heart of all we did. We got much greater buy-in from the team because the standards were theirs, and they believed in them.

I have always been a believer in the power of peer-to-peer accountability. Having your manager criticise you harshly can be easier to dismiss than if it comes from a peer. It is easy to feel like a manager is 'always having a go. They just spend their day in the office, they don't know what it's like – who cares what they think?'. If a colleague is telling a team member that they are making everyone look bad or that they are upsetting others, it is more likely to have an effect.

Part of our tribe mentality is that we want to be liked by our peers, and if you have to work with them day-in, day-out, the last thing you want to do is to annoy them. If the team has played a part in creating the standards, not only will they be more likely to uphold them, but they will self-police because they now have ownership.

To paraphrase Maya Angelou, how we feel when we are at work will always be one of our lasting memories; how we make others feel, one of our most significant legacies. Both of these are intimately tied up with the culture that exists within the workplace. Quite often it can be a series of small, seemingly insignificant actions that go on to have a huge impact. It is difficult to train this kind of attitude and behaviour into your team. Instead, leading by example goes a long way towards creating an environment in which your team members feel inspired and empowered to do the same.

# 3

# Communication

## Introduction

Excellent communication skills are central to your work as a manager. Quality of communication can make the difference between a great manager and an awful one. If you don't crack it (or are at least continuously work on improving it), your career could stall before it has even pulled out of the driveway.

This is the area that I see most frontline managers struggle with: you are being bombarded with information from above that you need to disseminate to your team. Often this information is poorly communicated to you, and has not taken into account the needs or perspectives of your team – nevertheless, it is your job to turn that information into action. There may not be a lot you can do about it, but you can make sure that your team is more inclined to listen to you and support you in your work.

(As far as I'm concerned, the secret to great communication is coffee – lots of it! Money doesn't make my world go round; it's a Kenyan medium roast enjoyed with colleagues as we put the world to rights and plan the success of our latest project.)

## Handling difficult conversations

The classic advice on this point is: don't put off difficult conversations. The key is to prepare, then take a deep breath and rip off the plaster. Delaying a difficult conversation makes things worse for everyone involved, and the stress of an impending conversation can be crippling. So, please don't drag it out.

Here are some key tips to help.

Before the conversation:
- Make sure you have done your research and have all the relevant information to hand (you don't want to get tripped up).
- Talk it through with a colleague – be careful here, as it is likely you will be discussing sensitive material, so pick the right person with whom to discuss it.

Planning the conversation:
- Pick your time – really, there is never a good time for a difficult, potentially upsetting or stressful conversation, so choose the best possible time and make sure that neither of you has to rush off, leaving the matter unfinished. These conversations will always take longer than imagined.
- Make it timely – ASAP is the basic rule of thumb. The longer you leave it, the tougher it will get. Leave it too long and it can become irrelevant and too late to tackle

(that is not a good thing, by the way – you haven't dodged a bullet). Not dealing with it means that it will only rear up and bite you at some point in the future.

- Choose your location carefully – somewhere neutral where you will not be disturbed. Make sure there are no unwanted distractions, that no one can overhear, and that the discussion is held in a safe space.

During the conversation:

- Make sure you give the other person a chance to talk, and listen to them.
- Be aware that the person may not be in an emotional state to return to their job immediately. Be prepared to give them a break or even send them home for the rest of the day, depending on the severity of the subject and how the conversation goes.

After the conversation:

- Write up your notes and share them with the other person (preferably by email) – give them the chance to discuss or suggest edits, in case you have misremembered any of the discussion.
- Be sure to sign off with: 'Please let me know if I have misremembered anything or you have any concerns. If I don't hear from you by [date] I'll assume you find the notes acceptable', as a lot of times you will not hear back from them. (Not recording things is something else you might come to regret.)
- Schedule a time to meet and catch up on progress.

## Tales over Coffee

My most memorable experience of a challenging 1-2-1 conversation was not one I was actively engaged in; it happened in a local coffee house. As I topped up my caffeine levels, I became aware of a heated discussion between two women (and that is being polite, although it had not quite tipped over into a full-blown row). I could see a number of the other customers in the crowded coffee house look up to see what the commotion was about. A few of us exchanged glances, we all tried to ignore it but couldn't help but look up again from time-to-time.

'I feel like you don't trust me, you're always reminding me to do things when I don't need reminding, like I'm going to forget.'
'You do', came the response.
'No, you don't give me a chance!' snapped the loud reply.

On the conversation went, and it wasn't long before I realised this was a work 1-2-1 between a team member and her supervisor. It wasn't going well, and in a busy public space – we all had ringside seats on a discussion about someone's performance. It felt like a piece of performance art, only it was very real and exposing an individual's and a company's private business.

After some to-ing and fro-ing about whether or not one felt trusted and the other had to explain how the company couldn't run on her needs, the supervisor started to turn it around. She emphasised how so much of the team member's work was really good, and it was a shame that one area of her work was letting her down. Gradually things calmed down, and the team member's threats to quit were forgotten – as far as I could tell, everyone was leaving happy.

As I got up to go, I looked at the hi-vis vest the supervisor was wearing: it was emblazoned with a company name and logo. Not only did I now know the ins-and-outs of their relationship and an individual's performance, I knew who they worked for, a whole range of office politics, and that clearly their supervisors had not been given any advice on sensible places to hold 1-2-1s – or how to behave when covered with the company's branding...

Sometimes, the conversations that you are most keen to avoid are the ones that ultimately will be the most productive. There is a reason you don't want to have them: a problem needing to be tackled, whether a poor working relationship in which you are avoiding someone, or perhaps an incident you don't want to have to deal with. Whatever the problem, if you are avoiding it, it needs resolving. After all, if you were not thinking about it, getting stressed or dodging it, it would not be an issue – there wouldn't be a problem to fix.

So, gird your loins and go fix it – then you can relax and get on with the fun stuff.

## The benefits of making time for coffee

I have always said that my career is built on a mountain of coffee beans. The first few months of any new job sees my calendar packed full of 'coffee with …' meetings, as I get to know new colleagues over a drink in a relaxed environment, building relationships that will benefit both parties in the future and see amazing things achieved.

Coffee in the less austere surroundings of a cafe is a running joke for many who know me, and I'm known for always having time for a coffee, but it plays a serious role too. A successful work life is built on people, and the relationships between those people.

---

### Tales over Coffee

In one job I took to basing myself in the cafe for the first half of a couple of days every week. Partly because the office I had been provided with was not fit for purpose, but also because I wanted my teams, who had a history of poor management, to see me as accessible. The rule was that if they saw me in the cafe and wanted a chat, they could pull up a chair, didn't need an appointment, and I would stop whatever I was working on.

I had lots of useful conversations this way, and it was time well spent (believe it or not, I also got a lot of work done between conversations – but then I'm someone who likes the sounds and inspiring distractions of a cafe when I work!)

---

It might be assumed by some that if a group of managers are seen laughing and enjoying themselves in a cafe they aren't working, but that isn't always the case. I held a lot of my meetings in cafes, and often encourage my managers to do so too (especially if I'm attending).

## Tales over Coffee

One of the most successful, high-performing teams I have managed was in the habit of going to the cafe on a regular basis. I would hear their laughter as they walked past my window. There were times when my entire management team had left the office. Phones would go to voicemail, and emails piled up in inboxes. And you know what? I didn't mind a bit. Some weeks it would happen a couple of times, some weeks it happened every day. As often as possible all of them would attend – on some days, one or two might be unavailable, but they were pretty consistent in their habits. Occasionally I would hear *'You coming, boss?'* hollered down the corridor – and if I had time, I would tag along.

The majority of the time those coffee breaks were spent discussing work: roughly 80% of the conversation was sharing ideas, asking for advice, making sure everyone was on the same page when communicating a particular message to the wider team. Sometimes, they were spent letting off steam and sharing concerns. When someone came back from holiday it was a chance for them to catch up with the most important news before they disappeared under the weight of their bulging inbox.

They could escape people dropping by the office, with that 'Have you got 5 minutes?' turning into 30 minutes.

Through small group discussions they were aware of each other's priorities, how much pressure colleagues were under and whether they might need some support, or indeed whether they needed to be left alone to focus on an upcoming deadline.

In the cafe environment they relaxed: the lack of an agenda led to a free-flow exchange of ideas (except when the time had been planned to discuss a particular topic). When the conversation turned away from work, they shared plans for the weekend. They commiserated over tales of expensive car insurance costs or celebrated birthdays. Occasionally they planned trips together on their days off to other heritage sites or galleries, sharing their interests. They laughed and exchanged banter, enjoying each other's company and simply took pleasure in their work and co-workers.

The workplace was somewhere they wanted to be, where they could spend time with people they liked. No matter how busy it was, I insisted they fit in a visit to the cafe.

To reap the rewards of this time together you need to be a cohesive, productive and ambitious team, able to make the most of this time and not waste it grumbling or, say, discussing the love lives of colleagues. You need to utilise the opportunity wisely. I gained great pleasure watching my frontline managers enjoy each other's company, knowing they would return to the office buzzing with ideas, to-do lists and a shared sense of purpose. Sometimes I would join them, but I also knew they needed time to plot how best to deal with the boss and get approval for their latest madcap idea. (And if they had the sense to return with a latte and a chocolate brownie, they were heading for success!)

## Put thought into written communication

In this age of electronic communication, our ghosts are stored on everyone's computer, and we don't want those ghosts to come back and haunt us. If you are annoyed, just take a breath before you write that email. Double check who is copied in – in fact, triple check who is copied in.

Store emails in an organised way. Get agreements on email – you will kick yourself if you have deleted an email in which someone agreed to support your project, and six months later they are denying it. It is also a great way to record any understanding you have come to with a team member, if your discussion did not warrant formal record-keeping. In Chapter 2 I talked about always doing the right thing: this extends to the way that you communicate with people. If you get it wrong in an email, then there will be solid evidence. There will also be the opportunity for a truly endless number of people to see your mistake first-hand.

Even in your emails you are representing so much more than just yourself. You hold a position of responsibility, and often will be speaking on behalf of others. Your electronic reputation is as important as any other.

---

**Tales over Coffee**

In a temporary job for a city council I once ranted to my boss in an email about a particularly unhelpful case worker. Sadly, I had hit 'reply all', and the case worker received my rant too.

Of course, there was no way I could hide from this, even if I wanted to – I had no choice but to own up to my mistake. Fortunately my boss liked me, it was a rare mistake on my part and he helped mop up the mess. I was lucky.

---

Having said all that, email is useful – but do pick up the phone too, drop by someone's office to answer their (emailed) question, if they are just down the corridor. Emails are easy, but they also make us lazy. Too often we hide behind our emails and text messages, avoid challenging conversations or simply cannot be bothered to get out of our chair – but that is not how relationships are built. Not to mention, it might take you 20 emails to come to a consensus with a co-worker when a quick conversation would accomplish exactly the same thing, and save you both time.

You can write a summary of what you agreed in an email so you both have a record, but it's helpful just to speed things up and engage properly with another human being.

## If you are unhappy, talk about it

'It's good to talk' was the tagline for the UK's British Telecom advertising campaign in the 1990s, it became a common catchphrase. Of course, this is true. I have lost count of the times that a member of one of my teams would come to me and complain about a colleague, the way they spoke to them or didn't respond to emails, or never answered the office phone, leaving it for others to do.

Sometimes the issues were more serious, and I would understand their frustration. In the early days of my management career I would try and find a way of discreetly raising the issue with the subject of their annoyance, while not dropping them in it. This was time-consuming and only caused me frustration; in some cases, it put me in an awkward situation, with a lack of solid or repeatable evidence. I just wanted everyone to get on, and wanted people to think that I could solve their problems, but over time I realised that this was an impossible task. Those involved simply needed to talk to each other.

### Tales over Coffee

I remember walking past the shared office of my management team one morning. Two of the managers were in there, talking – well, one was talking, and the other was crying:

'It's just that when you sent that email, you made me feel like …' was all I could hear from the non-crying one.

I carried on to my office next door, and left them to it. Why didn't I get involved? One had been frustrated by the other and she had decided, maturely, to talk it through. She wasn't raising her voice, she sounded calm and reasonable, and I knew the upset one well enough to know that she would listen and respond calmly. It was the advantage of getting to know my team well – I had a pretty good idea of how they would cope.

When I saw them later that morning, they were working together as normal with no signs of any issues – and neither had come running to me to solve their problem. Although these two managers no longer work together in their day job, they remain good friends and have collaborated together on a number of very successful projects.

Talking certainly did no harm – in fact, it made their relationship stronger.

If someone frustrates, upsets or does something to annoy you, consider the value of sitting down with them and calmly talking to them. If it does not go well and things do not improve, or if it is a particularly delicate issue, you can always discuss it with your manager – but please, have a go. If you are keen to talk to the other person but unsure how to go about it, you can ask your manager for some advice on how to approach the situation. You always want to be able to say that you attempted to solve the issue yourself first.

Whether the disagreement is between teammates or managers, and unless it is a particularly delicate issue, my response will always be the same: 'Have you spoken to them? No? Then talk to them about it, and come back to me if there's still a problem.' I have seen the culture and habits of teams change with this approach: it didn't stop team members approaching management with appropriate issues; it created healthier relationships, and lightened a little of the manager's load.

## Be careful who you complain to

There is another aspect of talking (or not), that a friend of mine wonderfully described as 'judicious venting'. In other words: be very careful who you let off steam to, especially as a manager privy to information that you should not be sharing.

Pick your 'ear' mindfully – especially if you have risen through the ranks, and those whom you used to confide in now report to you. Even with other peers, is your non-judicious venting going to leave them feeling like you are indiscreet? While they are nodding along, making sympathetic sounds, are they actually putting you in the category of someone they shouldn't trust? This is not to say that you have to keep everything to yourself and struggle through your challenges alone – just be careful.

Get to know people first, and ask yourself:

- Has it become clear over time that you can trust them?
- Have they kept smaller confidences you have shared?
- Have they been indiscreet and told you things that you shouldn't know (ignore the fact that you might have found it flattering to have been told)?

- Are they at a similar level to you in the company, and already privy to the kind of information that you might want to discuss during your conversation?
- Are they well-respected as a reliable colleague?
- Is it really appropriate to confide in them?

There are bound to be some things you really can't share with anyone outside a meeting or project team – in which case, *don't* (unless, of course, you think something unethical or illegal is happening, in which case follow the proper channels to raise concerns). Too many people succumb to the feeling of power that being privy to certain information creates, then wish to show that power by revealing what they know. Just quietly enjoy it: it will mean less to you as time goes on.

## Learning through silence

Shakespeare had it right when he said: 'Brevity is the soul of wit' (*Hamlet*, Act 2, Scene 2).

This is a general point, and relevant not only to frontline managers. However, it is a mistake that so many people make, and I want to make sure that frontline managers, who so often have the odds stacked against them, have this guidance to hand.

Generally speaking, the teams you represent are those who feel the least heard. There is every chance that they will not have been consulted in the early days of projects, and despite being a manager, even you might be powerless to make noticeable change. So when information is available to you, it is important to make sure that you take on board as much as humanly possible. Too many people don't get the benefit of the information out there because they are not really listening.

## Scenario

Have you ever been in a meeting and wanted to make a point, but are not getting a chance? Your point is relevant, and you don't want to miss your opportunity to contribute, but others keep on talking. You are no longer really listening, you just need to get your valuable point out there.

Then your moment comes. It is no longer quite as relevant anymore, but still important to you, so you say it. But it doesn't feel quite as satisfying as you thought it might. In another meeting you might experience this from the other side: sitting there quietly as people keep repeating points that other people have already made, or going off-topic. It is as though no one is listening to those around them, and the mission is just to be heard.

The same happens in 1-2-1 conversations. How often have you found yourself just waiting for the other person to stop talking, so that you can respond to what they said earlier? Your desire to make your point has become more important than listening to them.

Remember: silent is an anagram of listen!

Bringing an element of selflessness to meetings is key: if you have a fantastic point to make but someone beats you to it, that's OK, but do listen to what others say. Don't be the person resurrecting an old topic simply so that your voice can be heard. If you are going to repeat a point someone has already made, it should be because it genuinely needs repeating and you need to show support for that person: say clearly you are supporting them, it shows that you have listened.

If, by the end of the meeting, you have hardly said anything at all, that is not the end of the world – it doesn't have to be a reflection of your competence, it just means that all the important points were raised. A good chairperson will go around the table at the end of the meeting and ask each person one-by-one if they have anything to add. (Mind you, a good chair also will have shut down the ones repeating old topics, and made sure that quieter members of the group have had a chance to contribute.)

In your 1-2-1 conversations with people, just check in with yourself and ask: 'Am I listening? This comment I am desperate to make, is it essential? Can it wait?' Really good listeners are hard to find, so it is crucial to be one of them.

## Get to know *all* your team members

The size of your team may preclude you from taking each member for coffee (plus it might bankrupt you). But no matter how many, do communicate with them on a regular basis in a more personal way. For example, make sure you know and remember all their names (this might sound obvious, but I have come across managers who don't), and learn something about their lives. You can't put a price on the impact of being able to ask someone how their holiday was, which university their son or daughter chose to go to, if they are pleased with the new motorbike they bought.

Paying attention to them, showing that you remember and are interested in what they have told you, knowing if they are going through a tough time outside of work – all of this will make you a much better manager, and your job easier; plus you are likely to get a great deal of respect from them at the same time.

Moreover, your formal 1-2-1s with your team members are likely to be more relaxed and productive, after all, the icebreaking was done a long time ago and they will be more comfortable opening up to you. Believe it or not you also might find that, plain and simple, you just enjoy their company.

One of my jobs saw me being responsible for 150 people: the majority of them reported into my management team rather than myself – but I could tell you quite a lot about every single one of them because I took the time to chat to them. Even now, many years later, I am sure they would be pretty surprised by how much I remember about them! However, this isn't a one-off activity.

Building relationships is not just surface-level: asking a couple of questions doesn't achieve brownie points, nor should you consider the job done. If this is the case, you will lose credibility with your team pretty quickly. It has to be genuine, and being genuine means checking in with them regularly. Again, managing people means being interested in people.

---

**Case Study**

For a number of years I managed Claire Johnson, an excellent manager who has been employed by the Royal Collections Trust, worked at Hampton Court Palace and, at the time of writing, is working at Kensington Palace (an impressively themed career!). Claire is universally respected in her organisations, and has a real passion for training and development. The key to her success and positive reputation?

'I genuinely love working with people. I enjoy finding out their individual stories and experience; it also allows me to establish good working relationships with those I manage. In fact, I'm still in touch with a lot of people I have managed in the past, they're friends now.

I learned quickly how important it was to establish boundaries. I personally think it's very hard to be friends with those you manage while you are managing them, but getting to know them well is hugely enjoyable to me, and enables me to do my job better too.'

---

As much as I joke about coffee and give the impression that I spend most of my working days in cafes, there is a serious point to be made. None of us will meet our full potential if we try and work without the support of others – and in order to work together productively and cohesively, we need to build relationships and talk to one another. By this I don't mean passing comments in the corridor or a quick catch-up at the end of meetings, but sitting down with our colleagues, undisturbed, and really listening to one another.

We need to put as much thought into how, where and when we communicate as we do any other skills that are key to being a manager.

# 4

# Training Your Team

## Introduction

An essential part of any line manager's job is the training and development of their direct reports. If you were not to carry out this part of the job, not only would you be failing them but yourself, the company and your customers. Personally, I find it the most enjoyable and exciting part of my work. I love to see people grow and develop their skills. I enjoy watching people challenge themselves, and the pleasure they gain from realising what they are capable of achieving.

At its most basic, this is about making sure that your staff are given the right tools to do their job – to neglect this would be to deny a key part of your role. At the other end of the spectrum, you could be equipping the future CEO of the company to begin their own climb up the career ladder. Whatever your team's interests and ambitions, investing in their development will give you happier, more engaged staff who are much more productive.

However, if you are working with those who do wish to progress, it is important to note that it is not your job to make someone else's career happen. You can provide a positive environment, access to training and information, make suggestions and guide them. You might even make a couple of phone calls or call in a few favours from your own contacts. But do make sure you get the balance right, and that you are not doing the work for them. Apart from anything, it is good to test them. If they are genuinely keen and committed, they will start work on the actions you have talked about, they will take your suggestions and run with them (or be able to explain why they feel those suggestions aren't right for them, which is also OK).

Before you say 'I don't have a training budget, I can't afford to send my team on training courses', don't worry. If you don't have access to a budget, you might need to get creative with schedules and think outside the box, but not everything I am going to talk about here involves large amounts of money, or the authority to throw it around.

First, as introduced above, are you making sure that your team has the tools to carry out their job description? Whether that is customer service skills, manual handling, how to operate the technology or machinery that their role involves?

Once they have had that, it is not over. Too many managers think that if their staff have had training once, that is all they need; but in order to keep everyone performing at their best, people need refresher training. For example:

- Have there been changes in the industry for which they need training?
- Has the equipment they use changed at all?
- Has their job changed, and therefore their training needs to be updated?
- Has the organisation's focus shifted?

Once their basic training is done, there should be refreshers and reviews to ensure that they are on top of their game. Let's face it: anyone who says they remember and utilise everything they have learned on a training course is fooling themselves. Most people finish a course then return to work the next day, where it is business as usual – and a large proportion of what was discussed in the training is forgotten.

Training and development is not just about progression and promotion. It should be a continuous process throughout someone's time in their job. You are ensuring that your team is always fully equipped with the most up-to-date information and skills. The long list of benefits that this brings to everyone involved means that it should be one of the most enjoyable and valuable parts of your job.

## Having a plan

There are multiple ways of investing in the development of your team, but it's important not to take a scattergun approach, sending them to all sorts of different training sessions with no real plan or purpose in mind. Equally, their training should always be relevant and justifiable.

It is possible that your company has a development review process already in place. If that is the case, do make use of it – you will find it incredibly helpful. If not, then it is easy enough to put together a structured plan for the year ahead:

- Make sure that targets and tasks are aligned not only with team members' goals and aspirations, but also with those of the team as a whole, department and organisation.
- Assign responsibility for each task. For example, team members might be responsible for contacting another department to investigate the opportunity of shadowing their work for a day. You can arrange for other staff members to cover their shift, so they can be released from their usual tasks.
- Ensure you do regular progress checks.
- The plan may need to be amended over time, as team members' skills and needs evolve.
- Carry out a thorough review after 12 months, then repeat the process.

Ensure there is consistency in the way that team members are managed, especially if there is more than one frontline manager. Work with your management colleagues to ensure that team members are given the same development opportunities, and that you are all taking the same approach to supporting your team members. A well thought-out development plan will help motivate and focus your team members. It also will make your own job a whole lot easier.

## Tales over Coffee

Not long after starting a new job, I received a training request from a team member. They wanted to go on a photography course that the organisation was providing. The course was taking place during work hours, and I would have needed to pay the overtime costs of the person covering their duties.

The training had no relevance to their job, and the team member was unable to justify their attendance in relation to their role or that of the team, so I turned down the request. Almost immediately, a rumour started spreading around the team that the new manager 'didn't believe in training', but nothing could have been further from the truth. I am a huge advocate of training, but it does need to be relevant to the person's role.

In these circumstances, I tell people that they can go in their own time, if the training provider is happy with their being there for their own personal interest rather than for the benefit of the company. However, they must arrange to swap their day off with someone, so they can attend.

I will do everything possible to get someone on helpful, suitable training – I have even covered someone's tasks myself in order to free them up. But they need to work with me and show me how it will help them in their role, no matter how slight the connection to their day job!

## Training on a budget

Not everyone has huge training budgets, and often frontline managers do not have any real control over the budgets that do exist. However, if you are short on cash or struggling to get senior management on board, there is nothing stopping you from developing your own training programmes.

---

### Tales over Coffee

At Hampton Court Palace there was a fabulous range of training, but my team wanted something a little more bespoke – so the frontline managers put together some great seminars on creating CVs, interview techniques and career development across departments within Historic Royal Palaces.

I was always honest with people: the only career path I could personally advise on in any detail was a career in management. We gave those interested in a management career the chance to shadow frontline managers. If they showed initiative, they were invited to support their manager with some of the day-to-day duties, eventually stepping up into the role of 'acting manager'. Over time, some of them were successful in their application for deputy manager roles, and then manager.

---

You can pull in people from other departments to talk about how to get into their line of work (one of those times when building relationships and paying for coffee pays off); or if you have contacts, you can get a friend in from another organisation to talk on a particular subject (but be prepared to do the same for them in return).

---

**Tales over Coffee**

In one job where I had done a lot of change management work, I was asked to talk to other departments in the company about what was involved.

I was already on staff, so they didn't have to pay me anything extra, and colleagues elsewhere would learn from the first-hand experience of someone who had faced the kind of challenges they were likely to come across in the future.

All it cost the company was my time (which it paid for anyway), and my train ticket.

---

Another key source of learning for your team members is their own colleagues. Try pairing them up with fellow team members whom they can learn from in a structured way, with goals: perhaps something you are working on could benefit from the eye of a team member?

Your staff might be hungry for more to get their teeth into without any interest in climbing the career ladder. That is great – by all means keep them engaged, feed their appetite for greater challenges and more knowledge, but do avoid using it as an excuse to simply dump work on them that you don't want to do yourself. When there are projects that you can give team members ownership of, it gives them the chance to use their leadership skills. Be fair in assigning projects, ensuring that all team members feel they have the opportunity to prove that they can take on the work and succeed. Be sure to support them, and avoid jealousy and resentment from their colleagues.

## Tales over Coffee

Unfortunately, some of this work can lead to difficult conversations. I have been in the position where I managed people who were keen to progress and become managers, but could not take constructive feedback on board. They showed no noticeable change, no matter how much we helped them. The problems they encountered and behaviour they displayed meant that I could never promote them within our own team.

Not everyone is a good fit for a management role with responsibility for others, whether it is a personal style that they just cannot adapt, or a belief that they are always right. Sometimes they already have a reputation that means the best thing they can do is pursue a management role in another organisation: they have the skills, they are just not a 'good fit' for the team as a whole (see Chapter 1).

In one case I experienced, an individual's unwillingness and inability to take on feedback led to some very tough conversations with their frontline manager, then eventually with me as their senior manager. However, we were able to focus on

> this individual's strengths and steer them towards other opportunities for which they were far more suitable. Ultimately, they found their niche and really thrived in their new role.
>
> When it comes to development, be prepared to think creatively – as everybody is good at something.

## Identifying the right type of training

There is no doubt that some paid courses can be useful: for example, in my own career as a manager I have agreed the budget for team members and frontline managers to attend courses in a range of subjects including MAs, foreign languages, sign language and industry-specific short courses. But often, the more useful experiences came from finding opportunities in-house or using contacts outside the organisation.

Angela Qureshi, an experienced human resources strategist, trainer and coach, introduced me to the 70:20:10 Model for Learning and Development, developed by Morgan McCall, Michael Lombardo and Robert Eichinger in the 1980s.[6] The model sets out the most effective ways for people to learn leadership skills:

- 70% on-the-job experiences
- 20% from other people
- 10% from formal courses.

---

[6] Michael Lombardo and Robert Eichinger (2006) *The Career Architect Development Planner.*

If anyone on your team is interested in following in your footsteps, the best thing you can do is to find ways to help them out in-house. Of course, this involves finding ways to backfill their usual duties, and again, your response might be that you don't have the money to pay someone to cover them. But remember: if someone were to call in sick, you would find a way to manage it.

If you put the same thought into finding ways to get them valuable experience, the pay-off will be huge – it really is worth considering this. The benefits of having a well-coached, strong team will be invaluable.

---

**Case Study**

Joanna Hancox runs her own accountancy firm, Hancox & Co., in the north of England. She sends her staff on training courses, but also makes the most of a hugely effective and free resource in the office.

'I'll pair my staff up on some projects: a more experienced staff member guiding a less experienced staff member. Occasionally I'll have someone come and work closely with me in order to assist their development. I have found that not only is it a great way to increase the skills base in the office, but it helps bring the team closer together.

We really are like a family here, and everyone is keen to help and support each other – so I make sure to utilise that where I can.'

---

The training and development of your staff isn't about ticking boxes or paying for expensive courses. Yes, it's about making sure they have the skills to do their job and deliver the company's aims; but it is also about feeding their energy and enthusiasm, challenging them and giving them the opportunity to discover what they are capable of. They will feel like you care about them enough to invest your time and energy in finding new ways to engage and develop their skills (which says a lot more than just throwing money at a training course for them without much thought). You are telling them that you want to see them shine. That you believe in them, and that they matter.

## Training your 'invisible' team members

When talking about training and development, it is easy to focus on feeding the ravenous appetites of ambitious team members, but there is another group of people that we often forget about.

In Chapter 2 I talked about your 'backbone': those team members who have no desire to 'collect' training courses, get involved with projects or particularly challenge themselves. They will quietly go about their job and demand very little of you. That being said, they still need to attend the training courses that are pertinent to their specific role and are compulsory to everyone.

If you have taken on a team which hasn't received much in the way of training in the past, this is where backbones might struggle and show reluctance at getting involved. Yes, the training is compulsory – but do have a conversation with them about it, rather than simply putting your foot down. Some ego massaging will not do any harm either: remind them that they are hugely experienced at the job, and can bring unique insight to the training. Let them know that they can support those who have been in the role for a shorter period of time too.

If your company appraisal process requires you to set targets for the team, this is where your diplomacy skills really come into play, as you are bound to face a lot of resistance. Your backbone staff probably won't be interested in the courses you suggest or the new opportunities available, but there are bound to be things with which you can convince them to engage. For example, they might make superb work buddies for new staff, the perfect people to show their new colleagues the daily ins-and-outs of the role. If they love engaging with the public, they might be ideally placed to introduce customers to a new product, and so on.

Whatever you do, start small, and draw on your reserves of patience. Your backbone staff will never have long lists of objectives, but for them just a few small targets will be a great success – and it will be a massive achievement for you to have got them there.

## Using the skills already in your team

Don't be afraid of utilising the skills and knowledge of those you manage. Rather than a sign of weakness, it actually shows an ability to assess the performance of others – even when they are proving to be better than you at something – and to put the business before your own ego.

When recruiting, a good manager also will consider the range of skills that already exist within the team, including their own. When I think of high-performing teams I have managed, they have been well rounded due to a healthy mix of skills and experience, of which I too was a part. I would consider this when recruiting new managers, and what skills gaps we might need to fill.

Mary Wesson, an experienced healthcare executive in the USA, talked about a mistake that some less self-assured managers make: 'They are so insecure that they won't hire people smarter than they are: they want to be "the boss". I always hired people smarter than me – it made *me* look smart! Worked every time.'

That confidence comes with experience (the all-important 'miles under the belt' that I will discuss in Chapter 5), and will enable you to make important recruitment decisions. As you learn to recognise your own strengths and weaknesses, and accept that you cannot be great at everything, you will be able to step back, consider your team as a whole and make decisions based on the bigger picture.

## Giving performance feedback

Giving feedback can be as challenging as receiving it, only you are not necessarily the one who bears the brunt if you get it wrong. Feedback is an essential and important part of your role as a manager and you will be regularly giving it, good and bad, to the staff you manage directly on their performance.

Here are some 'dos and don'ts' to consider:

- Are you the right person to give the feedback? If you aren't, don't take this personally. Your end goal is for the recipient to hear the feedback and make changes. If they might take the feedback better from someone else, that is OK.

- Is your relationship a management or training one? If it is, then giving feedback is an inherent part of the relationship – you are not doing your job if you don't do it.

- If you are not their manager or trainer, ask if it's OK to give them some feedback. Bear in mind that they are perfectly entitled to say 'no' for a multitude of reasonable reasons (for example, they are having a bad day, they don't feel comfortable hearing it from you, they haven't the time to talk). Alternatively, you might decide that the right course of action is to talk to their manager and leave them to deliver the feedback or take further action.

- Is it the right time to give feedback? Your feedback should always be timely, and the general rule of thumb is as soon as practically possible. However, sometimes the best course of action is to wait, just not too long. Perhaps the recipient is under a lot of stress or very tired, so can your feedback wait for a day or two?

- Are you in the right location? Is it something better delivered away from your usual environment, perhaps in a more relaxed setting, away from others?

- Have you thought about what you are going to say? Make sure it is based on facts, examples or observations, and avoid vagueness. Ensure you have constructive suggestions for ways to move forward. Don't cover too many things at once, as this can be overwhelming.

- Make sure it is a conversation – that you ask for their thoughts and listen to them. Feedback should never be a monologue.

- Do you have enough time? Don't give feedback and dash off to your next meeting. They might have questions or concerns, so you need to ensure that you have the time to devote to this, rather than dropping a bombshell on them and running.

I have seen relationships destroyed by well-meaning but thoughtlessly delivered feedback. It's an essential and inescapable part of our role as managers, and can transform people's work and careers for the good, if delivered well. If you stand any chance of doing your job well, then you will have to give feedback. Learning how to do this in a constructive way, which comes across as helpful and not punitive, is important.

## Getting creative with staff development: a case study

Development doesn't have to be dull, whether someone is reluctant to engage with a learning opportunity, or trying to improve on an area which has been problematic for years. As outlined previously, it certainly doesn't have to be expensive, and often can be built into a current workload. Get creative, and you can have a lot of fun!

I was keen to develop the skills of a member of my management team at Hampton Court Palace, and a running joke provided an opportunity for him to discover his true capabilities. In post when I started, Dave Packer had begun his career at the palace on the frontline as a visitor assistant and eventually became a frontline manager – or, as he puts it, 'poacher turned gamekeeper'. He could have easily been one of the naysayers who resented my appointment, suspicious of change. Instead, he stuck by me. He became a 'temperature check' and had a good, level-headed approach to how the team might respond to new ideas and initiatives. I knew he didn't agree with everything I did, but we developed a wonderful working relationship based on respect, trust and a shared 18-rated sense of humour.

Dave could calm down an irate customer whose head was about to explode, he could deliver a last-minute tour to royal dignitaries and international politicians, but he will freely admit one area of weakness: his ability to keep on top of paperwork and administrative skills, which needed a little bit of work.

In order to get him to invest in improving this area, I set him an important task during one of his formal reviews (it was fully recorded and measured accordingly). As an organisation it was essential that we were prepared for any eventuality, but we had yet to create a key procedural document.

So I tasked Dave with creating the extremely important 'Zombie Attack Response Procedural Document'. For some weeks the banter in the office had turned to the best place to hide and how to protect yourself in the eventuality of a zombie attack on the palace. We had often joked that we should have a document that went into this. Well, we would joke no more! To say Dave grasped the project with both hands is an understatement, and well before the identified deadline, Dave handed over the most well-researched and thorough procedural document I have ever laid eyes on. It was a superb piece of work, and he would never be able to claim that these kinds of document were not his thing, or that others might be better at them. He says:

> It showed me that I didn't need to be worried about writing a procedural document or, for example, a risk assessment – the kinds of things I might have previously put off doing. If I can write 5,000 words for this, then not only is a risk assessment not a huge document in comparison, but it's not going to take long to create either. The idea of them became less overwhelming.

I always knew that Dave had good intentions, but just sitting down and getting started could be a problem for him:

I used to imagine that I had to sit down, start an admin job and finish it in the same sitting, which is almost impossible in our work – so things never got started, let alone finished. Through this I learned to make the most of my available time, and that completing a job over a longer period of time was fine, so long as I ultimately met the deadline.

But wasn't this piece of work ultimately going to be a waste of time – after all, the document could not be used beyond its initial creation, could it?

It was highly practical – OK, it was a piece of fantasy – but in order for it to work and be funny, it had to be anchored in real, practical considerations. So I had to take into account many of the same things I would with any other procedural document. My considerations and much of the research will be used again and again in future work.

There were other benefits for Dave that I hadn't considered:

Putting it into the Historic Royal Palace's [HRP's] 'voice' was a great exercise for me. HRP has a very distinct voice, and this needed to sound like an HRP document. It does, and in that respect is indistinguishable from other HRP documents – well, there are a few more pictures of zombies!

The beneficiaries went beyond Dave, and the document developed a life of its own that continues to this day. It was highly entertaining, and everyone was incredibly proud of what Dave had created – but we kept it within our team, sharing it with only a 'chosen few'. It almost became a piece of theatre, new managers being symbolically brought into the circle of trust by being allowed to read it in private, sworn to secrecy with regards to its content. As a result, it also avoided becoming a clique joke that excluded new managers; instead, it was a great way to introduce them to the humour of the team. At the time that Dave created the document it gave everyone a boost, and continues to do so, taking a place in the management team's folklore.

Dave discovered what he was truly capable of: that similar pieces of work could be completed around the demands of his job, that they were not onerous, and that it wasn't necessary to be daunted by them. However, most importantly, should the palace ever face a zombie attack, anyone within its grounds can rest assured that a comprehensive plan is in place – all will be done to keep them safe!

## Developing staff out of the business

As a frontline manager, it is not uncommon to be responsible for a team of people that includes employees who want to be somewhere else. Lots of people in frontline roles view it as a temporary post, no matter what the industry. Some might want more responsibility and a career in management, or to move sideways into different departments.

This can create a high turnover situation as it is, so why would you want to invest in their development when ultimately they are going to leave? Well, what if you don't and they stay? If you invest in them, then for the period of time they are yours, you will have motivated, enthusiastic staff who are committed to you, the team and the business. They will inject ideas and energy into their work, and energy and enthusiasm can be extremely contagious, positively impacting on many other members of your team. Do nothing and you will have frustrated, unmotivated, distracted people who are counting the days until they can leave, with no interest in bringing their A-game to work.

Steve Sargeant takes a similar approach:

> There's a strange stigma around looking for a new job, whether inside or outside your current company. In many organisations people feel it needs to be a secret, and I don't think it should. If someone has been on my team for a couple of years and feels like they are ready for the next step up, well, that's a success as far as I'm concerned. It should be celebrated.

Many of the management teams I have been responsible for could be considered prime, early-career posts, and usually I found myself managing highly motivated, ambitious staff. I could reasonably expect these managers to stay with me for approximately two years, then they would move on – that was fine with me. During those two years I had hard-working, dynamic managers, and my team thrived as a result.

Exactly the same goes for your frontline team members, whether they want to move up in the company, or head off elsewhere. Find ways to capture their knowledge and channel their Tigger-like bounce. Use their enthusiasm to your benefit, and that of the team. Embrace people's ambition and willingness to learn, or you could end up with a flat, sluggish team that does what is required to get through the day, but little more.

But how to capture this enthusiasm? There are a range of ways of harnessing their ambition and willingness to learn:

- Challenge them – engage them in projects which are a little outside their comfort zone. People can become bored if tasks are too easy.
- Find out what they are passionate about – is it a subject you can pull into a piece of work for them?
- Factor in their preferred learning and working style – you could diminish the enthusiasm of an extrovert if you give them a task that involves spending days working quietly in a library.
- Help them hone their natural skills – if they are quite vocal about what excites them, have them deliver training sessions or talks.
- See if there are opportunities for them to present to colleagues on work-related topics that get them excited – you could provide training for those unused to, or nervous about, speaking in front of an audience.

Whatever you give them, make sure that you are there to support and guide them, and remind them that it is OK to make mistakes, especially if you are taking them outside of their comfort zone. They will enjoy being challenged, but you don't want failure to knock them off course and dampen their enthusiasm. Try not to give a blunt 'no' to their ideas if you know they won't work under current circumstances; instead, explain why you can't follow up on their suggestions this time, and work with them to come up with something that is feasible.

## Tales over Coffee

In one job, team members were encouraged to deliver a morning briefing on a work-related topic of their choice. A 20-minute talk to their teammates was a great way to start if they were new to presenting, and we gave them training and support in the run-up to the presentation. Some went on to deliver their talks to other departments.

What of the task of recruitment that appears on a regular basis, if you take this approach? Even if your recruitment process is thorough, efficient and fine-tuned with practice, it can still be time-consuming – but it doesn't need to be stressful. Also, you should view it in a positive way. It is a chance to continue to form a team in the way you would like, plug skills or personality gaps, and provide an injection of fresh energy and new ideas. It's another opportunity to make the most of your people.

**Tales over Coffee**

One of the nicest things ever said to me came from Dave Packer at Hampton Court Palace, when a member of our team flew the nest for a management post in a different organisation: 'There goes another graduate of the Kate Minchin School of Heritage Management.'

Everybody involved – the 'graduates', their colleagues, the team, myself – were all about to face a new opportunity as a result of their departure.

**Case Study**

Meera is an operations manager with a large team:

'We always supported the development of our team, even if they really wanted to leave and work elsewhere in the company, or even elsewhere entirely. We never viewed it as a disappointment or threat. It's not uncommon for our customer services assistant role to be viewed as a way in for those who really wanted to end up in a different department.

Truth be told, once in our team they soon realise that it's not as easy as that, and they have a huge amount of work to do. But if they are prepared to invest a lot of their own time, sometimes money (they might need to study for qualifications in the evening or at weekends), take some knock-backs, spend some time working hard and developing their reputation, then the world can be their oyster.

Why doesn't this bother us? Well, if we tried to stall their development plans they would only resent us, they would become bored and unfulfilled. Instead, we have passionate, keen, energetic team members who help us out and contribute to the work of the team in wonderful ways.

As our customer services assistants start working in other departments, the organisation is increasingly populated by people who understand our work, challenges and needs. When I started in my role, other departments didn't want to go near my team: they were loose cannons who weren't being managed and no one wanted them. People weren't even keen to talk to them as a group – it was like facing a firing squad, let alone hire them.

Now though, and thanks to the work of the supervisors, customer services assistants are being employed across the organisation, they are being promoted into management roles here and elsewhere. The opinions of assistants are keenly sought, and they contribute to project teams. In very few cases does it involve using any of my training budget. We have to find ways to release them from their rota, and swap rest days sometimes, but the assistants are flexible – so are we as managers, so only for large-scale projects do I have to pay to provide staff cover.

We are all determined to make these opportunities happen, so we find a way.'

## The follow-up conversation

There is an important conversation that rarely happens between managers and their direct reports. It's a conversation that should take place after each training course they have been on, or the end of any project in which they have been involved. In this conversation you should be asking things such as:

- What did you learn?
- What are you going to do differently as a result?
- How will your experience support the work of the team and our customers/clients/visitors?
- Do you recommend others go on the course?
- Are you more aware of any other development you might need as a result of attending the course/completing the project?'

Of course, this doesn't have to be quite such a formal conversation. You can always take them for coffee and chat about it.

As mentioned previously, it's an unfortunate habit that we all fall into, no matter what our job: we attend a course and by the end of it, we are buzzing and full of ideas. The next day we get back to work and are immediately sucked into emails, issues and meetings: we have no chance to reflect or make a concerted effort to put into action what we have learned.

It can be really tricky for your team members who have to get straight back to work as soon as the training is over. You can help your team members avoid this problem by taking them away from their daily tasks for a little while and initiating the conversation. They will gain a lot more from the course this way, and you are likely to learn a lot too.

Training and developing your team members really is a no-brainer – it's also one of the highlights of the job. If you don't engage with this essential part of your role, not only are you limiting the possibilities for your team and the company as a whole, you are also limiting your own possibilities, as you miss out on a fantastic opportunity to practise essential management skills.

Invest some time and energy, get creative and you will see some great results. Moreover, you will gain an awesome reputation as someone who values your team, and respects their careers.

# 5
# Your Own Training and Development

## Introduction

A big part of your work as the manager of a team should be training and development, both theirs and your own. For you, whether you want to reach the top of your field and have more letters after your name than in it, or if you are happy remaining where you are and your only ambition is to receive a carriage clock on the day of your retirement, training and development still matter.

You owe it to your team and customers to keep your skills up-to-date. Sometimes this requirement will appear in your job description, but you should want to do it regardless. Often, there is an assumption that it is all about training courses, but this is far from the case. Besides, not everyone has access to these – certainly not through their employers. Moreover, the thought of paying a fortune to go back to university and study for an MBA can send frontline managers, who are on fairly low wages, cold.

However, the situation doesn't have to be about that. Some of the best ways of focusing on your own development are free, bespoke to you and can be done on-the-job. You would be surprised just how much can be achieved if you make time for coffee and read a book, watch a TED talk, or talk to someone about real-life experiences.

## The value of experience

It's not uncommon for (usually young) traditionally ambitious frontline managers to overlook a crucial part of their development. They are wonderfully keen, searching for the next project to hone their skills, keeping an eye out for the next job that will enable them to take a step up the career ladder. They attend numerous training courses, often take on postgraduate study in their spare time in order to get a highly prized master's degree or similar. (I have been there too, so I understand the desire to push yourself, learn as much as you can and move upwards.)

But while all this is happening, most people forget the most important and beneficial training there is: 'miles under the belt'. If you learn something on a course, then only use those skills once or twice, you haven't cracked it. You can't say: 'I know how to do that successfully, I have substantial experience of it now.' To be honest, you are not much further on than you were before you took the course.

As Michael Day comments, 'A lot of the really important experience comes from doing it again and again and again – and getting it wrong, and seeing how it works and reflecting.'

---

**Tales over Coffee**

I have a number of postgraduate qualifications, and have attended countless training courses over the years, but what was my most valuable learning experience? The six years in one role in which I was able to practise my skills time and time again. I introduced a great deal of change and saw it all the way through, out the other side and during a period of 'business as usual'. I worked on countless projects and saw the impact long after they were completed.

I have supported individuals through years of personal development, watched people progress and shine and, in a few unfortunate cases, managed people out of the business. I have dealt with my own personal issues and come through the other side much stronger. I have celebrated and commiserated with my team: we have had births, deaths and personal crises of all kinds.

None of this can be learned or experienced on a course or at a conference, or experienced and benefited from in such a comprehensive way in just a year or two at a job. Nothing is more valuable than gathering miles under the belt.

---

You don't have to take the traditional, upwards trajectory on your career path. Jo Killeya, an experienced project manager I was fortunate to work with for a number of years, says:

> Don't be afraid of moving sideways in your career. Sometimes, moving into another industry or a slightly

different role within the same industry can provide that invaluable depth of experience, rather than climbing the ladder too quickly. The air is quite thin at the top.

My own career, for example, has had a number of sideways moves. My aim has never been to get to the top as quickly as possible, but to take on work which excites and inspires me, develops skills and gives solid experience with real depth. I would never have gained all that if I had simply leapt from one rung of the career ladder to the next, sights set firmly on a corner office and expense account.

## There is nothing wrong with qualifications

Don't get me wrong, I am not against academic qualifications or traditional training courses – as mentioned previously, they have featured heavily in my own career. All I would say is: think carefully about the timing. Be sure that you will benefit at that point in your career, and that you don't dismiss other important development opportunities.

When interviewing potential frontline managers, unless there is room in the team for an inexperienced manager who has real potential and the capability to develop, companies will be looking for:

- evidence of experience;
- projects seen through to the end;

- challenges faced and overcome; and
- skills that have been practised and honed.

It is simply not possible to replace all of that with a master's degree. If you are certain that you do want to head down the academic route, then Aileen Peirce, Head of Interpretation and Design at Historic Royal Palaces, has some great advice:

> Think hard about what you want to do before shelling out thousands for an MA, and do proper due diligence on the MA course, thinking like a consumer rather than an applicant. Ask lots of questions about what jobs the graduates have got afterwards, and don't be fobbed off with a list of employers without specific job titles attached. Is the MA helping people get graduate-level jobs – or did all those people get jobs with a great organisation, but they're actually on the till in the gift shop?

Sign up for a postgraduate qualification because you are genuinely excited by the subject. A course of study is a massive time and financial commitment to embark on just because you think you should, only to find yourself miserably slogging away to the end – especially when there might be more interesting, useful and unusual ways to increase your experience and bolster your CV.

## Take time to reflect

One particular theme emerged from many of the interviews I carried out with frontline managers for this book: very few of them ever got, or actively sought to get, time to themselves – a chance for some headspace and to reflect.

Being at the beck-and-call of a large team demanding attention, responding to the demands of senior management, and being called on to talk to customers and resolve their problems – frontline managers still have to respond to emails and phone calls while, in some cases, carrying radios that have to be reacted to immediately. They usually share noisy offices with limited or zero access to private space, are on rota patterns beyond their control, and have to take lunch breaks when they can – if they get them at all.

More often than not, it feels impossible to find time to stop and think, reflect on your own performance and figure out how to cope with the challenges of the job. However, finding the time for this is essential, and not achieving this is something that more senior managers see as impacting negatively on the overall performance and development of frontline and early-career managers.

When we go charging from one meeting to another, try to clear our inbox as quickly as possible while simultaneously taking phone calls, we don't get time to step back and think. For example:

- How did the last briefing you delivered really go?
- How responsive was your audience?
- What would you do differently next time?

How about the 1-2-1s you hold with your team members:

- Is the format working?
- Are you really listening to them?
- Do you have any new ideas that might motivate them further?

Have you supported a busy colleague enough? How did you handle a performance issue? I'm guessing that you take 10 minutes at the most before sitting down with someone. Here, I am not talking about planning an agenda or reading over old notes, but *real thinking time*: to reflect and consider, allow ideas to drift in and out.

If you are part of a team of managers, give each other time to reflect: this is one of the most powerful gifts you can give each other. Look at your diary and identify days when one of you can be spared for the morning. If you are thinking, 'We can't – we're always short-staffed', what would you do if one of you were taken ill? You would make it work. So you really need to make it work now: this is important.

I have managed some of the most hard-working, overstretched, under-resourced management teams, and with some imaginative thinking and forward planning (and sometimes calling in a favour or two), we have always managed to fit in some individual or group time to reflect. Ensure you all get time to clear a few hours in your schedule, go and find a cafe (yes, have a coffee!), far enough away that you will not be disturbed. If you are not allowed off-site, find an empty room and put a 'Do Not Disturb' sign up. If you are one of those left behind with the extra workload, it is only for a few hours and your time will come.

Try and make this a regular thing, and remember: time out to reflect and think is *not* a luxury. It is an essential part of performing at our best, and in turn essential for our teams, the company and our customers.

So yes, take the time to go for a coffee with colleagues and get to know them better so that you can work better together – but take yourself for a coffee too, it really is a crucial part of your development. Take a book, take this book and notepad, think about what you want to try doing differently in the future. Think about what you are already doing well and how to keep it up. Nancy Kline has written a fantastic book, *Time to Think: Listening to Ignite the Human Mind* (see Further Reading). Get hold of a copy and read it on your next trip to the cafe – it will be hugely relevant to your work with teams.

This issue is not just about how you can deliver the practicalities of the job to an even higher standard. How often do you stop and think about your own experience?

Does your work excite you?

- Are you increasingly tired?
- Are you frustrated in your role?
- Do you really know why?

Time to reflect is also time to listen to your gut and think about the bigger picture. There might be small adjustments that you need to make in your role:

- Perhaps you need different challenges?
- Maybe you haven't realised how much a difficult relationship with a colleague is bothering you, and you really need to work on it?
- It might be that you have found a project that really inspires you, and want to give more of your time to it, because it makes you get out of bed in the morning?

These are the kinds of feelings and experiences we don't allow ourselves any time to consider (except perhaps when we are catching up with a friend outside of work and let off steam – cathartic, but not hugely productive). Be kind to yourself: you are not a machine. If you are finding yourself regularly ploughing your way through the day, it's OK to stop. It isn't a waste of time to make time for yourself.

This might sound like a ridiculous indulgence – particularly the bit about heading off to the cafe with a book! – but apart from the likelihood that your quality of work will improve, you also stand a chance of maintaining your sanity.

## Seeking even more experience: projects

The key here is to get involved. As Aileen Peirce says:

> Get experience. It's really easy to get tied up in the day-to-day pressures of your job, but try to take opportunities to expand your horizon. If there's an interesting project, get involved, help out on a different team, cover for a superior – if there's a chance to do an interesting training course with people from other departments, then take it.
>
> Gaining varied experience and building a network across the organisation is critical for long-term development – so seize your chances to do this.

If you want to stretch yourself, develop your CV, ensure the voice of your team is heard (and often for frontline teams, that means correspondingly the voice of your customers), find opportunities and get involved in projects beyond your day-to-day responsibilities.

It may well be unusual to have someone in your position on a particular project team, but there is no harm in asking: it illustrates interest, willingness to learn and puts you on other people's radars. That being said, you cannot pursue a project 'just because you fancy it'. The project manager needs to see the benefit of having you on board, both for yourself and the team. Once there, you are now the representative for what can be a very large group of people. You need to be engaged, do your research and contribute appropriately.

Aileen Peirce again:

> I think that younger staff in particular feel they have to accept existing ways of doing things, but actually what I'm interested in is how to do things differently and better. So, speaking up in meetings, having the confidence to suggest something new and the evidence or thought process to explain why it's a good idea will absolutely be welcomed, and they shouldn't stay quiet.

> The mistake that is sometimes made, though, is offering subjective opinions without any evidence to back them up. For example, the classic 'visitors think', which can translate as 'a visitor once said they didn't like X – and because I personally agree with them, I'm extrapolating from that sample size of one and have decided it applies to 600,000 people'.

> However, it might mean: 'I've stood in that room watching visitors for five years, and I've rarely seen anyone engage with that [thing of choice], and I wondered why. So I must have talked to 20/50/100 visitors because I was intrigued to find out, and I think the reason for their lack of interest is …' – then it's incredibly useful information that could change the course of a project.

Joining a team of experienced, often more senior colleagues, can be incredibly nerve-wracking, but don't worry. First, there is a strong chance that there will be others in the meeting who are new to this. Second, if you have any choice, select your project carefully. Try and find one with a project manager who is welcoming and known for running things well. Meet with them before your first meeting, to find out more about the project and how they go about organising things. Ask about what contributions they will be looking to you for, get a feel for their style and personality.

We don't always have much choice over the project we get involved with, so if this is an optional thing – a passion project – again, do your research and choose wisely. Once on board, spend some time with some of the other project team members. By now it won't surprise you that I suggest buying them a coffee and finding out more about their role on the project, so that you understand their needs and responsibilities. Don't forget, this is another opportunity to get your name out there.

Here are a few other points to remember.

- Make sure your own manager is on board with you taking on this extra work, if the project is outside of your normal remit. If you don't run it by them first, you could encounter some difficulties.
- Once you are involved in the project, be mindful of what you are learning and how that knowledge can be applied in a larger sense.

- Don't forget that you are representing a potentially large number of people – how are you going to gather their views and relevant experience, then distil that into useful information for meetings? How are you going to feed back to them following your meetings?
- Make sure to find the time to reflect on your experience and truly benefit from it.

As Angela Qureshi says:

A major project is a really fertile learning ground, so long as you reflect, you pause and think: 'What have I learned from this?'

For each aspect of the project, ask: 'How did that go?' – and can you get feedback from others involved on your performance? It doesn't have to be formal.

Joining a project team, even just for some development experience, is a lot more than just turning up for a few meetings and sitting quietly in the corner. It is an opportunity to develop your skill set and become known as a valuable asset to your company.

## Working with a mentor

Another low-cost and hugely beneficial development opportunity, which you can organise yourself, is having a mentor.

A mentor is a trusted advisor, someone more experienced than you with a strong reputation in their field. They can help guide you, they will ask questions to challenge you and make you think. They are not there to give you all the answers; rather, to provide support as you find your own. They might be able to point you in the direction of opportunities, whether a training course or jobs, and help you think through what you might need to do to improve your chances of getting either. However, to be clear – it isn't a relationship where the mentee expects their mentor to get them a job, or introduce them to important people.

Mentors do not have to work in the same industry as you, let alone the same department, although it is useful for them to have an understanding of your line of work. They will be able to bring a valuable alternative perspective; also, having to explain some of the basics from time-to-time can help you bring clarity to a problem that you are trying to solve.

How to find a mentor? Some organisations have in-house programmes, pairing people up from around the company. You might have met someone at a networking event, or a colleague might be able to recommend someone.

---

**Tales over Coffee**

I have had a couple of different mentors over the years: two were assigned to me through workplace programmes, while another was introduced to me by my company CEO who wanted to support my career and pulled in a favour from an old friend.

In all of these cases, we would meet for coffee every couple of months, occasionally scheduling in an additional meeting if I had a particular problem that I wanted to talk through with them. I found all these relationships to be incredibly helpful.

---

I spoke to Mike Sarna, an independent museum and heritage consultant, who was my first mentor, for his thoughts about being both mentor and mentee:

> When I've sought a mentor, I have looked for someone who would really push me, make me think and rethink things, that 'critical friend'. When I'm mentoring someone, I'm always pushing them to trial new things. I try to get people to understand different styles of working within complex working environments.
>
> I've learned so much from being both the mentor and mentee – regardless of which side of the relationship I am on, I have always found the exchange hugely valuable. I find it all comes down to a few things: feeling empowered, gaining confidence, and a sense of authority. Everyone wants to perform well at their job,

and we as organisations put up so many barriers. I find the mentor relationship extremely fulfilling in supporting working through those barriers, and building confidence.

---

**Tales over Coffee**

One of my mentors would regularly ask me 'Why not?' when I quickly concluded that something would not work. In the process of explaining 'why not' I often realised how weak my argument was, how often I made assumptions, and how little excuse I had not to give something at least a go.

It wasn't always a very comfortable thought process to go through, but it was illuminating and useful.

---

Choose your mentor carefully, and make sure they have the experience to be able to support you in the way you need. Get to know them before you consider them as a potential mentor. You should get on well with them, and feel that you can trust them, as it is important that they can be honest with you and challenge you. Sometimes you might not like what they have to say, but you should listen and discuss it with them. Ideally they will push you beyond your comfort zone, so it is better not to choose someone too similar to you. (I would recommend reading *One Minute Mentoring* by Ken Blanchard and Claire Diaz-Ortiz – see Further Reading – as a great introduction to all of this.)

Having a mentor isn't a huge time commitment in your diary, although you will need to dedicate additional time to reflection both before and after your meeting. It does not need to cost any more than a couple of coffees (yes, you should always be buying!), but the positive impact on your own development can be huge.

## Seeking feedback on your performance

Now, here is a tough one. It's important to create a culture in which people feel comfortable holding each other, and management, to account. In a similar vein, you really ought to seek feedback on your own performance. Even if only as part of an annual review process, taking a temperature check on how you are doing is key. Admittedly this is hard: no one likes asking for feedback, for fear of being told what an awful job they are doing; but it is important your team knows that you aren't asking them to do anything you would not be willing to do yourself.

This is all part of the bigger-picture work that you are hopefully doing, to create a culture in which people know how to deliver feedback constructively and considerately.

### Tales over Coffee

I still find receiving feedback incredibly hard and have been known to avoid asking, but I have experienced the benefits too.

I have been lucky enough to head a management team who felt comfortable enough giving me feedback when I had frustrated or upset them. I'm sure they didn't find it easy, and walked past my office door a few times before actually coming in and talking to me. In one instance a young member of my team in his first management role had the guts to tell me when I had annoyed him. It turned out that his point was completely valid, and indeed I had been out of order. I had to swallow the feedback, put my hands up and learn from it.

I admired him for having the strength of nerve to challenge his manager. He was polite, respectful and made his point clearly. He gained a whole load of brownie points that day – I was hugely impressed (and a little sheepish!).

Some organisations have opportunities to receive '360-degree feedback' from a number of colleagues in a structured way. This should be done with the backing of your manager, who works with you to utilise the feedback; but also you can do it informally, asking people who interact with you in different situations for constructive feedback on both things you do well, and areas on which you might need to work.

If you do this, make sure that you are ready to hear the feedback, and be prepared to do something with the information you receive. Being open-minded and taking in constructive feedback can be a challenge. If you are nervous about the process, have a conversation with your manager. If you have something along the lines of a learning and development department, have a chat with them. As previously mentioned in Chapter 4, feedback is important, but if delivered thoughtlessly or requested in the wrong way, it can be upsetting and set people back rather than move them forward.

---

**Tales over Coffee**

I once asked a manager for feedback on my performance. I explained to them that I had been receiving some really nice, unsought compliments from colleagues, but I was keen to hear their view of my performance.

I was expecting something along the lines of: 'You've done a great job on project X, but I need you to give more focus to project Y', or some such. Instead, they said: 'Yes, there have been some positive moves forward, but this holiday you leave for tomorrow, I know you booked it before you even applied for this job, but it's inconvenient – I need you here.'

That was the sum total of the feedback. I was gobsmacked. I had been feeling pretty good about my performance (and, so it seemed, were many of my colleagues), and yet my manager pulled me right down: the comment was neither useful nor constructive – I could do nothing with what they had said. My manager had just taken from me any of the positive feelings my colleagues had instilled in me, as well as the associated energy and enthusiasm. Instead, I was left upset, confused and demotivated.

In contrast to that, and while in the same job, I was sharing coffee with a colleague one day when she asked if I minded if she gave

---

me some feedback. This was an experienced colleague whom I respected, and I was happy to hear her thoughts. We sat on an extremely senior management team together, and it was my first time in such a senior capacity.

'When we're in our board meetings, you don't need to be so apologetic. You have a great deal to contribute, and you were hired because of your knowledge and experience. You belong there as much as anyone round the table. You sometimes start your comments with "I'm new to this, but I would suggest …", or "I've never considered things at this level before, but in my opinion …" You are weakening your argument by being so apologetic or excusing yourself, and you should be more confident.'

She was right. I was in the habit of saying things like: 'I don't have as much experience at this as some of you, but I think …' I have never forgotten her constructive, evidence-based feedback, and she changed an aspect of my behaviour for the good. I will always be grateful to her.

Your own development is a career-long project: every piece of work, every project, every conversation is an opportunity to learn and develop. The important thing is taking the time to reflect, and to increase the benefit that you can gain from all the hard work you are putting in on a day-to-day basis.

# 6
# How to Be a Manager: the Bigger Picture

## Introduction

Being a manager is about so much more than the practical aspects that appear in your job description – in fact, quite often the most important elements of your work don't appear in your job description at all. As a result it can be a real challenge to work out how to be the best possible manager, and easy to make mistakes along the way.

It doesn't matter where you are in your management career, whether in the early stages or in post for 10 years: it can be possible to remain uncertain about these less obvious aspects of your work, and even trickier if you have not been fortunate enough to have great role models and mentors. It might be that you have not had access to training, or have been unsure where to seek further guidance.

If this is you, don't worry! Some of the things that you might have struggled with, or been confused by, are actually perfectly normal parts of the job. They are also things that can trip people up who are much further along in their career, so this is not about your inexperience. That is one of the joys of this kind of work: you are never done learning, and continuous evaluation and reflection can be a source of great discovery and enjoyment.

I outlined previously how frontline managers so often get caught up in day-to-day work, and so the topics covered in this chapter are some of the most common areas to be missed (or worried about) in the rush and hurry of daily work. A lot of what I will discuss links back to the concept of getting miles under your belt – but it is possible to get a head start.

## Don't try too hard

'Aspiring leaders who attempt to mimic their heroes make a fatal error. The point is to be more like yourself, not more like someone else'.[7]

One of the most common mistakes I see is people trying to 'be a manager'. Whether they have an idea of what a manager should be from books, TV, managers they have had over the years or just conclusions they have come to over time – if someone is trying to 'be an image of a manager', you can spot it a mile off. The work persona doesn't quite fit with the real them that you recognise them to be. It is like putting on someone else's coat

---

[7] Rob Goffee and Gareth Jones (2015) *Why Should Anyone Be Led By You: What It Takes to Be an Authentic Leader*, p. 203.

which doesn't quite fit. They struggle with the grey areas, as these don't fit neatly into how they thought things happen for managers. They are trying too hard to be something they are not, and struggling to reach an ideal that does not exist.

This is a really tough position to be in – after all, there is no one way to be a manager, and the best managers are those who show us their personality, not a cardboard cut-out.

Steve Sargeant has come across managers struggling with this:

> I've worked with a number of managers who are fairly new to the job, and they come in to it with a sort of 'Right, now I'm the manager and I know everything' approach. Of course, they're faking it because they think that's how they ought to come across, what people are expecting of them and that being uncertain isn't allowed. But it's not helpful or healthy, and I would encourage all managers to be open and honest about their strengths and weaknesses.

> Talk to people about what you're thinking – ask their opinion if you're not sure how to move forward with something. So much of what we do is a dialogue, and working with people requires a conversation, openness. The managers I've greatest respect for are those who are the most open with their teams.

## Authenticity and confidence

While researching this book I returned to Hampton Court Palace to meet with David Hingley, my line manager while I worked there (since our interview he has moved on to work at The Landmark Trust). Over coffee in the palace cafe, and with his radio chattering away in the background, we talked about authenticity and how some people struggled with 'being a manager'. Between us we had gained a lot of experience guiding younger frontline managers. We watched them grow and gain skills, make mistakes and pick themselves back up again, stepping in where needed and giving advice where it was wanted (and sometimes when it wasn't, but they needed to hear it).

I asked David about the challenge of going into a new role and 'owning it', making it your own when you don't have much experience: perhaps your first management role. It is not uncommon for anyone who is nervously approaching their first day on a job to be told: 'You've no need to worry, you've been hired because of your skills, knowledge and experience, you'll be fine!' Yet new managers can have limited skills, knowledge or experience compared to their colleagues, so how do you get through those early months with some self-assurance?

David feels that:

> It's really hard. I think it's about getting the balance right between having the confidence that you do have some of those skills, but also having the confidence to

acknowledge the gaps in your knowledge. There will be staff who are going to test you, push you and see how you react. The best response is to say: 'I haven't been here as long as you, I'm thinking of doing X – can you share your experience with me, and let me know what you think?'

You shouldn't reveal that you're not confident, but you should be honest enough to say that you don't have all the answers. I think people don't resent that as much as they resent someone pretending to be confident and stamping their feet when they want something done – that just leads people to shut down on you.

I have talked about the need to apologise in Chapter 2, and asked David about making mistakes in front of new teams:

I'm a big believer that most people don't want their manager to fail, because life is a whole lot easier if you've got a good manager.

So it's about getting some of the older, more experienced team members on your side to give you the benefit of their experience – and also because then, they'll quite often talk to some of the rest of the team and occasionally say: 'Cut them some slack, they're new, they're trying.' You need voices and support like that, and it's a bit arrogant to assume you'll get by without them.

At the palace, David and I established teams with strong personalities and wonderful camaraderie. We wanted our team members and managers to enjoy their jobs, to feel that they could come to work and be themselves, but describing what that looks like can be tricky. Again, this is an area where it is easy for people to make mistakes. As David explained:

> I'm very happy being an older manager now. As a younger manager you read all the books, people tell you how to behave, you attend lots of courses, and you end up with this 'managerial version' of yourself which doesn't necessarily 'fit', because it's not you. It's really not easy – especially when you're young – as you're doing it against a backdrop of your own personal development. So it's worth accepting that it's going to take a while to figure out who you are as a manager.

> Maybe start by deciding what type of manager you're comfortable with being. Are you good at getting everyone on-side? Are you quick-witted enough to get people laughing, but still deliver the big messages? Are you the guru everyone comes to for advice? Are you brilliant at remembering all the important stuff?

> You need some sort of strong base to build out from. Whatever your management persona, it has to be authentic – so it needs to be you at the core. This all gets a lot easier as you develop a greater understanding of 'you', and I don't think you can just learn it.

David builds on this:

> Earlier in your career you're very concerned with making sure you have all the skills of a manager, and you are viewed as competent in the role. As you get older and potentially move up in an organisation, you and your job conflate more as your leadership role develops. People have decided they want a particular sort of leader – so when you're recruited into a post, they've taken you on for being you, not a competent manager. They've assumed you are a competent manager.
>
> In my early management jobs, so long as I had good skills and got on with people, it was OK. As you move up, the authenticity starts to get more important because people are looking up at you. It's interesting: as a younger, junior manager you're less exposed in some ways, so you have the opportunity to work out how you want to be.

With that, David's radio crackled into life and he was called to respond to a problem: an extremely senior manager, yet today his work life was dictated by his radio. That's life for operational managers!

Over the years we worked together, David and I have spent a lot of time drinking coffee, reflecting on the challenges we were facing at the time, talking about how our staff were developing and performing, but also about what *we* were learning, dissecting our approaches to things. We are both still learning, but we have been in the game long enough to stop worrying quite so much about who we are.

If you are still in the 'angst stage' and trying to figure it all out, feel free to stop giving yourself such a hard time. Your team and colleagues want *you* rather than a version of you that you think is expected – and that includes the 'you' that is learning and making mistakes as you go.

## The risk of overconfidence

It is worth saying a little more here about confidence, which goes for everyone – no matter where you are in your career journey. Keep an eye out and make sure that your lack of confidence doesn't actually show itself as overconfidence. That in trying to make up for known gaps in experience or skills, you go into overdrive and end up coming across as arrogant. Avoid overplaying your position of responsibility (or power, if you want to look at it like that): you don't have to behave like 'the boss', because you are the boss! You do have the upper hand, the authority, the ability to make changes and affect people's working lives – it is inherent in your role, so no need to shout about it.

Even if you don't always feel it, calm, quiet confidence will get you the respect for which ultimately we are all hoping. It shows that you are in control, and that in itself is a hugely valuable skill.

Wave your position around like a badge of honour, and people will doubt and distrust you.

## Allow yourself to be human

Far too often, managers think that they are not allowed to be human, to display the signs that tell their teams they are having a rough time, or just say it out loud.

Vikki van Someren from The Bike Shed talked about the positive impact of not hiding the reality of your life when managing others:

> In business, people are always trying to be textbook-perfect – but we're all human beings. We all have bad days, we all have family problems. We all have issues, and actually being open and honest is going to create a much healthier work environment than trying to pretend that everything's perfect, you're amazing and you've not got any faults.

> I actually think that those who can be mindful, aware of their own emotions and thoughts and express those healthily, are stronger leaders. You're better at reading the environment and your effect on it. It's very valuable self-awareness. If you allow yourself to be human, you allow others to be human too – you'll have a much greater bond with your team, and a much healthier working environment.

Chip Conley, who founded the Joie de Vivre hotel chain, says a similar thing in Dorie Clark's great book, *Reinventing You*:

> Being authentic and vulnerable helps me, and it helps others be vulnerable with me ... If you think your boss is above emotions, above having difficult times ... then that's going to make you feel like that's what you're going to have to be yourself. And if they feel like 'I can't do that', it diminishes their ability to live up to their potential.[8]

As we touched on in the previous section, no matter where you are in your management career, you will have spent time considering how you are viewed as a manager, and what kind of manager you want to come across as – the risk is in overthinking it, and attempting to manufacture an idealised version of what you think a manager *should* be. At which point, you are really just setting yourself up for failure.

Take a step back, recognise the strengths you already possess, and build on those. Again, accept that it could take years to figure out what kind of a manager you are, and what your management persona is. So take the pressure off yourself and enjoy the ride.

---

[8] Chip Conley, in Dorie Clark (2017) *Reinventing You: Define Your Brand, Imagine Your Future,* p. 151.

## Compete with yourself, not your colleagues

More often than not, frontline managers are part of a team of frontline managers. Between you, you manage a large team of frontline staff, and you all report into the same manager. If you are not part of a team in this way and you work alone, I am sure there will be numerous managers across the organisation at a similar level to you.

Having access to a group of people in the same position as you, facing the same problems and challenges, can be hugely beneficial. You have a self-made support group of people who immediately 'get it'. However, there are some who turn this into a negative, and view their fellow frontline managers as competition: for a place on the next exciting project team, the next training course and, most significantly, for the next promotion, maybe even their manager's job.

The problem with this strategy is that no matter how much incredible work you try and produce in order to wow everyone, your motivation is your own success, not that of the team or company. Your focus isn't the customer, it is the corner office or the fancy job title – and as a result, your work will not be as good as it could be. Moreover, people will soon figure you out, and the end result is that they will always be questioning your motivation: their trust and willingness to work with you will diminish. What about those who do stick with you, in spite of this? Either they are seeking associated glory by hanging on to your coattails, or they hope to use you to skip up the career ladder themselves eventually (and possibly even overtake you). Not great people to have on your side.

The only person you should be in competition with is yourself. Each day, try and be better than you were the day before. Challenge yourself, take the time to think about what you are doing, how you are doing it and how you could do things differently next time. In competing with your colleagues you are losing the benefit of a valuable resource and truly being a part of a team – both of which will go on to benefit your development far more than viewing others as rivals ever will.

Everyone is good at something: everyone has their own expertise from which others can benefit, just as you have experience and skills that you can share with them – and gain a reputation for being a real team player in the process.

Claire Johnson, the team leader we met in Chapter 3 with a 'royal' CV, told me what helped her most in the early days of her management career:

> It was my colleagues, no doubt about it. I had the privilege of working alongside two other amazing managers and an excellent line manager above me – all with a lot of experience. Between them, they showed me how to be a manager: I often reflect on how lucky I was to have them around me to show me the way. They all had very different styles, which allowed me to develop a well-rounded style of my own.

I will always be grateful for their guidance and support in the early days.

Being in constant competition with those around you is exhausting. While others are enjoying the productivity and pleasure that comes with a collaborative approach to working with their peers, engaging in one-upmanship benefits no one – least of all yourself.

## Choose your battles wisely

One of the most useful phrases I have ever been introduced to is: 'Don't die in a ditch over it.' In other words, pick your battles.

During our career we will encounter many things that we are passionate about, and whether we want to fight the corner for ourselves or for others' benefit, sometimes the best thing to do is to negotiate. Meeting those who disagree in the middle, taking a completely different approach to the problem, stepping back but holding on to the information for a future occasion, or just walking away completely, might be the most productive course of action instead.

Sometimes the need to walk away can be because the issue at hand is rather small in the grand scheme of things, and you need to save approaching a particular senior manager or committee for when you have a much bigger problem to take to them. Sometimes it is simply that you are never going to win: all the time and energy you could spend fighting that battle will be wasted, energy you need to use elsewhere. Also, you just don't have the time to take on every possible skirmish that crosses your path.

Sometimes, the situation isn't even about realising that we are not going to win an argument; rather, that simply walking away from a winnable battle is the right thing to do. Perhaps you need to help someone save face, or you want to raise a different, more important issue later on and need everyone to be focused on that instead.

---

**Tales over Coffee**

In one role I desperately wanted to change the job titles of a group of supervisors. The new title I was seeking would have better represented the work they were doing, and been a well-earned upgrade.

Although I understood some of the arguments against this move (nothing to do with their performance, the issue was the impact on parts of the wider organisation), it was still something about which I felt strongly.

After writing a business case and talking to a number of senior managers, eventually I realised that my argument was going nowhere – so I settled for an alternative title as a compromise. To this day, I still wish I could have got my team the new job title, but ultimately, backing down from my original argument and meeting them in the middle was the right thing to do then, and remains so now.

---

You may well find that communicating the end result to your team presents you with a further challenge, especially as you might not be able to tell them all the factors behind your decision for reasons of confidentiality and/or company politics. Hopefully the majority will trust your decision making, or come to understand further down the line why you have made those choices. Some will never understand, but that can be the way with management. So long as you are confident that, with all the information to hand, you have done the right thing, then indeed you have done the right thing.

## Don't use all your management tools at once

We aim to have as many skills as possible to help us with our work, but sometimes those tools can be a hindrance rather than a help, if we are unsure when the best time to use them is, or if we overuse them.

### Case Study

Margaret is a machinist for a fabric manufacturer. She was approached by her manager and spoken to about her performance.

'I was in the wrong, but I felt lectured at. I've been doing this job for 20 years – I'm happy to admit when I get it wrong, and I don't need to be spoken to like a child.'

Margaret outlined everything her manager had said to her – he had used a long list of recommended techniques and questions:

'Can you tell me why I might want to talk to you?'
'Can you understand how the other person might have felt?'
'Can you tell me what the wider impact of what you said might be?'
'What would you do differently next time?'

The week before, the manager had been on a performance management training course and his contribution to the conversation sounded like the training notes. Margaret was a long-standing, experienced, mature member of staff. She was far from perfect, but good at her job:

'A quick chat to pick me up on the mistake would have been fine. I'd have said that I was sorry. That I realised afterwards how stupid that was, and I wouldn't do it again. But instead I was left feeling stupid and angry.'

There was no need for a 15-minute lecture, to treat to Margaret like an 18-year-old in her first job, or the team member who never seems to listen. Her manager only needed to use one or perhaps two of his newly-learned skills, which would have been enough. Instead, he upset and alienated a good, experienced employee, and would now need to rebuild that relationship.

The manager above made the common mistake of being taught something and then using all the information at once. Whether you are on a training course or reading a book, all the tips and techniques you are learning form a 'management toolbox'.

For example: if you are building a shelf, emptying your toolbox on the floor and insisting on using everything in it for the job, whether or not it is needed, obviously would not be practical (or appropriate). Instead, employing the two or three tools that are the most useful for the situation and leaving the others where they are, will help you achieve the desired result. It is the same with the 'tools' you gather as you learn to be a manager.

Angela Qureshi has an interesting approach to this:

> I try and get people to see these tools as lenses through which to view a situation. It gives you a couple of perspectives through which to work out what to do, or how to approach something. If it doesn't feel authentic to you, then you can adapt them or try something else.

Being keen to learn is fantastic, but the challenge is not about taking on as much information as possible and viewing yourself as an 'expert'; the real challenge is knowing when to use that information and adapt it. Otherwise, you will make people feel like you have literally thrown a book at them, and they will be too dazed to learn anything.

## Speaking on behalf of others

Once you are working at management level, you are no longer representing only yourself and your opinions. Now you speak for an entire team, your customers, and often other stakeholders. You have been given a voice that you might not have had lower down the organisation, a place at the table. However, going into meetings and voicing an opinion that is yours alone is unwise: you need to do your research. Sometimes, this also means voicing an opinion that is opposed to your own.

There is no harm in an appropriate discussion to say that you have concerns and explain them, but *personal* is what they are. Never claim your opinion is that of others, unless you know for sure that they agree. How to do this? You might have a team of hundreds, and customers of hundreds of thousands. Talking to people – not all of them, obviously – is essential and this is where hiding in your office becomes a way of neglecting an important part of your job. So, walk the factory floor and talk to your staff. Join them in the break room from time-to-time. Work alongside them or on the shop floor. Get to know them, their concerns and expectations. If you manage an enormous team, spend time with as many of them as you can, but put in place representatives who do much of the legwork for you.

The same goes for your customers. Your team members can get an excellent view of their opinions, but you should gather some first-hand knowledge. Being able to sit in project meetings and say: 'I've been speaking to a number of customers …' is not only helpful to the project but makes you look good, that you have your finger on the pulse.

Your multiple voices include that of the organisation's management team, of which you are also a part. No matter where you rank in the company structure, whether your job title is 'manager', 'supervisor' or 'team leader', you are now part of the overall management of the company. This is where many frontline managers come unstuck: there will be situations where you are unhappy with a management decision, but you have to communicate it to your team. You don't agree with what's happening, you might feel that a project is a waste of money, or you feel frustrated by what your team is being asked to do by those more senior than you – but you still need to deliver the message.

I have witnessed managers in this situation say things such as:

'I don't agree, but I have to tell you all to do X'
'I agree with all of you – this is crazy, but we have no choice'
'I'm not happy, but I've been told to tell you …'

Of course, this is in no way appropriate, and even those you are trying to appease will see it as unprofessional.

I talked to Michael Day about the challenge of becoming a manager and having to communicate a message you don't agree with – he and I are on the same page:

> Frontline managers have a duty – a contractual duty –
> to operate their managerial practice within the context
> of what the organisation wants to achieve. It's
> irresponsible to take a management role and then
> undermine what the organisation is working towards.

If there are aspects of the decisions you have to communicate that you disagree with, then by all means find some constructive ways to challenge them in normal debate and dialogue. If you're being asked to do something that appears unachievable or won't work in practice, then clearly constructed feedback is appropriate: 'I really want to do this, but I'm finding it hard because ... can we have a conversation about that?'

---

**Tales over Coffee**

I have found myself in a number of situations where I disagreed with decisions that had been made – and more often than not, others also shared my views. I communicated my concerns and the likely reaction of my teams, I talked to the relevant people in order to express my views and try and gain further understanding of what had been decided. But in many of those situations, I simply had to accept what was happening.

---

You have to know when to draw the line and know when there is nothing further you can do. No matter how passionate you feel, at the end of the day it is a job, and you are paid to carry out the work of the organisation. If you find yourself in a situation where you really cannot support the actions of the company or carry out what is asked of you in a professional manner, then it might be time to look elsewhere.

As Angela Qureshi says:

> You can say: 'I have done all I can and it's not acceptable, and therefore I am moving on. It might not be quick, but I'm going to find my way out.' Or you can say: 'I've done all I can, it's not acceptable but I would rather stay than move on.' You've made a positive choice to stay and put it to one side.

> Ultimately we have a choice – people for all sorts of understandable reasons forget they have that choice or are afraid to use it, but it's available to us.

In accepting a management role, you have to accept certain consequences, as Michael Day explains:

> If you take on the role of manager at any level, your mindset has to be 'I'm a manager'. In accepting the challenge of being a manager, you have to be prepared to say: 'I'm accepting that I have a duty of care to the team I'm managing, a responsibility to them to do the best I can – they need managing, and managing well. I have a duty of care to the people I report to, to implement the things we all agree we are trying to do, and I have a duty of care to my organisation and its stated goals – what it hopes to achieve for its customers.'

There are myriad reasons why people accept the offer of a

management role, but it is important to remember that in doing so, you now represent the voices of countless others – and that sometimes these will conflict. It is a delicate balancing act, but one that is achievable.

## Keep up the networking (over coffee)

Coffee – yes, that magical bean! I have said it before, and I will say it again here as it's worth repeating: build relationships, find time for coffee, take the time to chat away from your ringing phone and the endless stream of staff who appear at your door.

You are part of a much bigger team now: theoretically, you always are, whatever your role – but many companies struggle with an overall team ethos, and people find themselves working in silos. It's time to do all you can to break out of that. You are part of multiple teams now, working on different projects, sitting on different committees. Managers quickly become part of multiple management teams. You speak with many voices and listen with many ears (and, indeed, wear many hats). Having a strong network of colleagues across the organisation will only make you a better manager. Just as I talked about the necessity to carve out quality time with your management peers, you need to build the same positive relationships with colleagues elsewhere.

**Tales over Coffee**

In previous roles, there were certain people with whom I would set up monthly coffee meetings. It didn't matter whether there were any pressing concerns or not, it was simply important to spend time with them, knock ideas about, ask for advice or be a sounding board for each another.

Our paths would cross on a regular basis in meetings, and it was helpful to understand the views and perspective of someone else at the table, as well as to know I had an ally.

## Do your homework

You really need to be fully prepared for many of the additional responsibilities you have taken on, and the much broader knowledge you require as part of a management team. This might seem like an impossible task when you are trying to fit it in around the demands of your team and those of your own manager, which is a full-time job in itself. But I promise you, taking the time to prepare will bear fruit. Getting up early to fit in coffee with a project manager before work, or to have the office to yourself and do some research before a meeting might sound hellish now, but in the long run it will pay off.

It is essential to make sure you understand your organisation's cause, strategy, goals and missions (it may have more than one, and different companies call them different things). Also, to be sure that you are aware of your team's role in that bigger picture.

For example:

- What are the company's current big projects?
- What is it focusing on?
- How much money is it investing?
- Who has it partnered with?

Do you know the answers to these and other similar questions? You need to be able to talk the language of the company and to be able to start using it, if you want to achieve anything that requires the support of those outside your immediate sphere of influence.

When you attend meetings, think about who is sitting at the table with you. Is it human resources, maintenance, finance? What are their priorities? What are their schedules and workload? If you are not sure, find out by networking with them and speak their language when you are in meetings with them. You stand a much better chance of getting invited back to the table and being able to play an active role if you understand how they operate, what pressures they are under, when their busiest time of the year falls, and when they are most likely to have the time to help you out, should you need their support.

Getting to know your peers in other departments and understanding how they work can be a real benefit when you are facing a problem, or there is some kind of crisis. As well as having an enjoyable working relationship with them on a day-to-day basis, you can give them a call, explain that 'I know that this is an awful time to ask, but could you by any chance …?'. You never know – they might just do a favour for a colleague they know, who cares enough about their work and priorities to learn more about them.

However, this is not simply about earning, banking and distributing favours: it should not just be a transactional relationship; rather, simply because you like helping people out, building relationships and would not ask for help unless you really needed it. As I have emphasised throughout this book, the reality is that to be truly successful, we cannot work in a silo (although heaven knows some people try, and some even manage some adequate output – but they will never set the world on fire!).

All of this work – understanding others, your role in relation to them and the company as a whole; building relationships, contributing to meetings in a fully informed way – marks you out as someone to be taken seriously. It can save you a lot of time and stress too.

### Tales over Coffee

I have had frontline managers asking me to pursue an issue for them, fight their corner on a problem on which they were not gaining any traction. They would be frustrated by another department's lack of engagement with something that was bothering them. My own knowledge of other departments enabled me to know whether to take on their issue.

I knew:

- whether to use my seniority to try and move things forward;
- whether or not this was the wrong time to try and fight this particular battle – and if not, then when was a good time to take this on; and
- how to frame the problem to align more closely with the department's own priorities.

This is all knowledge that you can gain for yourself: you don't need to rely on your own manager to do this for you. You can be equally as informed – then when you do call on your manager for support, you will know that it is not only a good use of everybody's time, but more likely to result in other departments paying attention and being up for a discussion.

## When 'it'll do' is good enough

When it comes to getting it right, there really are 'it'll do' moments. This might not sound very professional, but it is realistic. To put it another way: 'Done is better than perfect.' There will absolutely be times when you just have to get the task done. You need to be careful, because it is experience that will teach you how to identify these moments. It might mean juggling priorities, which results in a particular piece of work not being perfect, but that is OK – it is more important that something else is.

You just have to pick your moments, and the recipient of the work (probably not the best approach when doing work for the

CEO, your most valuable customer or, say, preparing for a royal visit!). But I assure you, there is a time and a place.

## The grey areas of management

I have talked about 'grey areas' a few times in this book: well, here they are again. Learn to relish them and view them as a place of learning and creativity, where your staff are at their most 'humanlike'.

When you are managing people, nothing is ever black-and-white: you will learn so much by navigating your way through those grey areas and embracing them fully. To my mind they are one of the best bits of the job – which is handy, as they are inescapable. As Michael Day says:

> You need to accept the challenge of 'I am a manager' and relishing all that means. You can't do it reluctantly; you can't do it half-heartedly. You might do it badly sometimes and get it wrong, but you have to want to do it.

The staff I have worked with who wanted to become managers, and who ultimately decided it wasn't for them, usually came to this conclusion because they could not cope with lack of certainty. They wanted one solid answer to their questions, one resolution to issues, but I could not give that to them – it's impossible.

This is why getting to know your team and colleagues is so important, why you should keep on top of your skills and knowledge, why you should be genuinely interested in people and why you should get those miles under your belt. None of this will give you that one definitive answer, because it doesn't exist – but it will make it a lot easier for you to make the right choice, at the right time, for that particular set of circumstances.

## Look after yourself

> 'In the event of an emergency,
> oxygen masks will drop down in front of you …'

We have all heard this safety announcement on an aeroplane. It goes on to say that you should put on your own mask before assisting anyone else: after all, what good are you to them if you haven't made sure that you have enough oxygen to help them in the first place? It is exactly the same when you manage a team.

Often, there is something lost in all of this – you. I don't mean in the 'letting your personality shine' kind of a way that I have discussed earlier, but your health and well-being. Everyone wants a piece of you: you will find yourself being manager, counsellor, parent, referee and, to repeat Frances Sampayo's wonderful description in Chapter 1: 'psychiatrist, life coach, guru, keeper of all answers, solver of all problems and reasons for all problems'. You are bound to end up tired and stressed, and while you are busy trying to look after everybody else, the only person who can look after you is … you!

Make sure you get enough sleep, eat healthily, take exercise. Get up from your desk and take a walk around the block. I am sure you feel like you are expected to be a superhero, solve everyone's problems, be everywhere at once, do the job of three people – and that is just in work. Add to that whatever you have to deal with in your private life, and it's a wonder that your head doesn't explode. It is OK to walk away sometimes, to have had enough, put your pen down and get out of the office for a little while for some fresh air.

It's important to know that you will not always get it right, and that you cannot fix everyone's problems. You need to be able to build up the physical, mental and emotional resilience that will get you through every kind of day, good and bad. You cannot keep supporting your team and working hard for their success if you don't think about how to best provide those things for yourself.

Almost everyone I interviewed talked about the importance of taking a break and getting some headspace. Claire Johnson told me:

> I wish I'd known early on how important it is to establish a good work–life balance and stick to it. Once those lines are blurred, it's very hard to say 'no' to staying a bit longer or working an extra day here and there in order to help out.

Frances Sampayo commented: 'It's hugely important to take a lunch break and have time out. Even just 20 minutes of having the phone muted, no emails popping up and just a bit of time to reflect can do wonders.'

Jo Killeya talked about a common mistake among new managers trying to make a good impression:

> They work too hard, and by this I mean long hours, building up an unusable amount of TOIL [time off in lieu]. They don't have time to take their annual leave and end up being exhausted, unproductive, difficult to work with, and generally gearing up for a nervous breakdown.

David Hingley was reminded to put things into perspective: 'The best advice I was given at an early stage of my career in retail was: "On a good day, it's a multimillion-pound business. On a bad day, you manage a shop."'

Never be afraid of asking for help if you are struggling with any aspect of your job. It doesn't have to be a technical issue; it might be the workload, or the stress you feel after dealing with a particularly challenging staff problem. Hopefully you will feel able to talk to your manager or human resources department. Talking it through alone might help; alternatively, they might be able to direct you to employee support programmes.

Often, supportive colleagues or managers are enough to get you through the tough patches, but sometimes they are not and you need to seek help and advice elsewhere. Whatever it is you need, please look after yourself. You have a duty of care to yourself, not just your staff. Sometimes *you* need to come first.

Looking after yourself isn't just about the tough days. Make sure you take time to focus on all the great stuff. Celebrate your accomplishments, pat yourself on the back, and be sure to recognise when you have done a great job. It might just be reaching the end of a recruitment process and on-boarding a promising new team member. You might have found out that you are going to get new uniforms for your staff, or perhaps you have received a lovely email praising a member of your team.

Even the small things are worth raising a glass (or cup of coffee) to. Life is short, and full of a lot more joy than we often realise.

# Conclusion

The skills covered in this book are important in *all* management roles, whether you are just starting out or the CEO. Sadly, you will not always see these skills being demonstrated at every level, but you can lead by example with your own team. As you progress, good practice will progress with you.

You don't need an MBA to be a good manager – none of it is rocket science. As I have emphasised in this book, being genuinely interested in people and helping them to meet their full potential is key: whether team members, colleagues or customers. At the core of every great manager is care and consideration for those you manage, and with whom you work.

So, what are your next steps? Clearly, you should be heading out for a coffee and taking time to reflect! Consider which areas of the book you feel you need to give greater thought to, then create an action plan for yourself. For example:

- Perhaps you need to spend some time considering your own standards and those of the team as a whole. How are you going to develop those standards, and use them to help get the best out of your team?

- Do you have a personal development plan in place, or do you need to work on one with your manager? Do you have personal development plans in place for your team members?
- Are you really listening in meetings and 1-2-1 conversations?
- Are you engaging the disruptors in conversation? If not, how are you going to get that started?
- Is it time to invite your manager for coffee and get to know one another a little better?

Spend some time getting on-side those whose support, approval or assistance you need to turn your plan into action, then off you go. Take time to consider your progress and where you might need to change tack as things develop. Don't forget to thank those who help and perform well as you go. Then last but not least, make sure you celebrate the milestones along the way.

Over the years I have watched team members develop in ways that even they didn't think possible to pursue their own career dreams. I have watched young managers gain confidence as they made mistakes then picked themselves up, determined to do better next time and go on to do even better than they imagined they could. I have seen seasoned, cynical professionals become the most energetic contributors to a new piece of work. I have been involved in project groups that have resulted in superb products and events. I have also been involved in a fair few committees and teams that had me mainlining coffee to stay awake and considering jumping out the window – but in hindsight, I am very pleased that I was there to serve as the voice of others. Even when things have gone a bit awry, there is a huge adrenalin rush that comes with finding solutions and not only fixing things, but making them even better than before.

Managing others and taking on the responsibilities that come with that is a real honour. You might have days where this really does not feel like it, but I assure you it is. Team members, colleagues, your manager – they are all looking to you to make things right. They are putting their trust in you, and you would not be there if someone, somewhere, didn't think you were capable of it.

I certainly feel very honoured to have played my part in supporting others and contributing to the work of some amazing organisations, but it is all thanks to the people who were prepared to give up an hour of their day and have a coffee with me. I have learned more from these people than I have on any course. I have laughed and cried over more cappuccinos than I will ever be able to count. Projects have been conceived and finalised over mugs of foamy lattes and paperwork stained with coffee rings. Young managers have picked my brain, and my own mentors have dispensed invaluable words of wisdom.

My career really has been built on a mountain of coffee beans – or more accurately, on the advice of those who were prepared to have a coffee with me.

There is nothing more enjoyable and valuable than sitting down with a colleague and learning from each another. As a result, you should always have time for coffee.

# Bibliography

Clark, Dorie (2017) *Reinventing You: Define Your Brand, Imagine Your Future*, Harvard Business Press.

Goffee, Rob and Jones, Gareth (2015) *Why Should Anyone Be Led by You? What It Takes to Be an Authentic Leader*, Harvard Business Review Press.

Harvard Business Review (2014) *Frontline Managers: Are They Given the Leadership Tools to Succeed?*, analytic services report. Available at: https://hbr.org/sponsored/2016/04/frontline-managers-are-they-given-the-leadership-tools-to-succeed (accessed 1 November 2018).

Lombardo, Michael M. and Eichinger, Robert W. (2006) *The Career Architect Development Planner,* 4th edition, Lominger.

Proto, Eugenio (2016) 'Are happy workers more productive?', IZA World of Labor, December. Available at: https://wol.iza.org/articles/are-happy-workers-more-productive (accessed 22 October 2018).

Sgroi, Daniel (2015) 'Happiness and productivity: Understanding the happy-productive worker', Social Market Foundation, Global Perspectives Series 4, October. Available at: www.smf.co.uk/wp-content/uploads/2015/10/Social-Market-Foundation-Publication-Briefing-CAGE-4-Are-happy-workers-more-productive-281015.pdf (accessed 22 October 2018).

## Further Reading

Behar, Howard with Goldstein, Janet (2007) *It's Not About the Coffee: Leadership Principles from a Life at Starbucks*, Portfolio Penguin.

Blanchard, Ken and Diaz-Ortiz, Claire (2017) *One Minute Mentoring: How to Find and Work with a Mentor – and Why You'll Benefit from Being One*, Thorsons.

Cain, Susan (2012) *Quiet: The Power of Introverts in a World that Can't Stop Talking*, Penguin Books.

Chapman, Bob and Sisodia, Raj (2015) *Everybody Matters: The Extraordinary Power of Caring for Your People Like Family*, Portfolio Penguin.

Green, Alison (2018) *Ask a Manager: How to Navigate Clueless Colleagues, Lunch-stealing Bosses, and the Rest of Your Life at Work*, Ballantine Books.

Hadeed, Kristen (2017) *Permission to Screw Up: How I Learned to Lead by Doing (Almost) Everything Wrong*, Portfolio.

Kline, Nancy (2013) *Time to Think: Listening to Ignite the Human Mind*, Cassell Illustrated.

Kline, Nancy (2015) *More Time to Think: The Power of Independent Thinking*, Cassell Illustrated.

Kouzes, James M. and Posner, Barry Z. (2003) *Encouraging the Heart: A Leader's Guide to Rewarding and Recognizing Others*, Jossey-Bass.

Kouzes, James M. and Posner, Barry Z. (2007) *The Leadership Challenge*, 4th edition, Jossey-Bass.

Porath, Christine (2016) *Mastering Civility: A Manifesto for the Workplace*, Grand Central Publishing.

Watt, James (2015) *Business for Punks: Break all the Rules – The Brewdog Way*, Penguin.

# Acknowledgements

Huge thanks go to everyone who has contributed to this book and supported me through the process.

To all of my interviewees, not all of whom wished to be named. Kitty Caisley, Mike Finneran, Joanna Hancox, Agata Hardin, Aurora Heimsath, Claire Johnson, Jo Killeya, Christian Lax, Christopher Lentz, Lynne McCormack, Michelle McCormack, David Packer, Aileen Peirce, Angela Qureshi, Pat Raikes, Steve Sargeant, Mike Sarna, Becki Scott, Dil Sidhu, Vikki van Someren, Liam Stanley, Susan Stark, Todd Tucker, Mary Wesson, Matthew Yates and Victoria Yates.

Some very talented people have helped make this book sound better and look better than it would otherwise have done. Thank you to my editor, Lisa Cordaro, and to Michael Day for his kind and thoughtful foreword; Heather Fitz, David Hingley and Frances Sampayo, who kindly provided comments on earlier drafts of the manuscript.

I am extremely grateful to my friends and family who took this project seriously from the very beginning and supported me in so many ways. My wonderful parents, Eileen and Allan Minchin, have encouraged me, no matter what journey I have chosen to embark upon. My amazing wife, Sue, who believes in me more than I believe in myself.

To everyone who has taken the time to join me for coffee over the course of my career, thank you.

# About the Author

Kate Minchin began her career producing and directing fringe theatre, before moving into operations management in theatres and arts centres in the north of England where she first experienced managing teams on a large scale. After completing a master's degree in cultural policy and management, she moved to London where she managed multiple teams at the Natural History Museum in the education and operations departments.

During her time working for Historic Royal Palaces, Kate was based at Hampton Court Palace, leading a team of visitor services staff and their managers. While there she worked on one-off events such as the Olympic cycling in 2012. Kate also worked on projects that ranged from creating a wine-dispensing fountain to recreating a historic kitchen designed solely for the production of chocolate.

At the University of Oxford's Ashmolean Museum, she was Head of Operations: her responsibilities included the visitor experience, security, building maintenance and health and safety.

Her major interest and motivation has always been ensuring that her teams receive high-quality training and support in order to perform at their best, as well as the opportunity to develop their careers in whichever direction they are most passionate about.

Kate now lives in the New York metropolitan area with her wife, Sue. Together they ride motorbikes all over the world, and drink far too much coffee.

www.kateminchin.com

37590264R00108

Made in the USA
Middletown, DE
04 March 2019